DISCIPLINES FOR LIFE

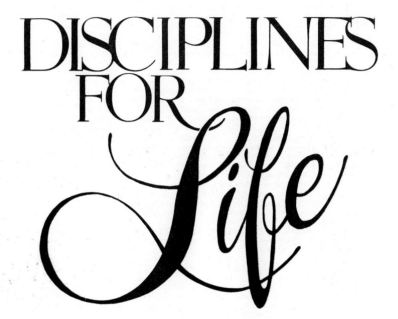

DISCIPLINES FOR *Life*

Lance Webb

THE UPPER ROOM

Nashville, Tennessee

Book and Cover Design: Nancy Johnstone
Cover Transparency: Frances Dorris
First Printing: May 1986 (5)
Library of Congress Catalog Card Number: 85-52020
ISBN: 0-8358-0539-5
Printed in the United States of America

[Deliver us] from the toil
Of dropping buckets into empty wells,
And growing old in drawing nothing up!
—William Cowper

CONTENTS

Preface   *9*

Part One
The Need for Disciplines of the Spirit

1. Two Ways to Life   *13*

2. Buckets for the Well of Life   *25*

Part Two
How to Understand and Use the Disciplines

3. The Basic Disciplines of True
   Perspectives   *37*

4. The Costly Disciplines of Illumination   *71*

5. The Joyful Disciplines of Acceptance   *96*

6. The Disciplines of Caring Love   *140*

Notes   *169*

PREFACE

In this fresh and rich and honest book, *Disciplines for Life*, Lance Webb has poured out his personal odyssey in the spiritual life. Beginning with great frankness about his own and his daughter's lives, he draws upon the agony and the ecstasy of living a disciplined Christian life. He illustrates this not only by his personal disciplines but by a rich collection of experiences that figure after figure in our own generation have shared.

With ever-renewed experience that in Jesus Christ God has come all the way downstairs, Lance Webb witnesses to the piercing love of God that never ceases to draw upon our hearts if, through discipline, we are made open to receive it. Those of us who know Lance Webb have seen him carrying on the work of his older Methodist colleague, Albert Edward Day, as a principal guide of the Disciplined Order of Christ. We have seen his influence in the fascinating Methodist experiment implementing the very disciplines described in this book by initiating a program that, in its first outreach, has brought some forty-eight persons from across the country to Nashville, Tennessee, for eight five-day sessions over a period of two years in what has been called an Academy of Spiritual Formation.

Lance Webb has not only been an effective spiritual guide himself, but in his later years he has written several books on a variety of subjects. His fictional work concerning the apostle Paul, the slave Onesimus and first-century Christian life is not only historically sound but makes the century come alive and quickens the reader to the costly but decisive shaping of the Christian witness. Few bishops in the Methodist or any other church have been more humbly effective in sharing their witness to both the agony and the ecstasy of a disciplined Christian life.

DOUGLAS V. STEERE

Part One

THE NEED FOR DISCIPLINES
OF THE SPIRIT

1

Two Ways to Life

The big boys dragged the skinny, timid, "preacher's kid" by the heels over the basketball court until they wore out the seat of his pants. At the same time, they were also leaving wounds in his psyche: the hurt of their rejection gave him a deep sense of inferiority and a loss of self-worth. One result was to cause him to stutter, and this led to even greater feelings of worthlessness and embarrassment. As he finished high school and went to college, he could begin a spoken sentence that started with W only by saying, "And . . . what do you want?"

That scared, bashful boy was I, Lance Webb. I was the thirteen-year-old son of a New Mexico Methodist circuit rider preacher. He had been my first teacher in a one-room school in Boaz, New Mexico, in which there were only a half-dozen or fewer children other than my brother and two sisters. As long as this idyllic existence continued, I remained secure and happy. But then we moved to Tatum, New Mexico, where for the first time I encountered the cruelty of other children. I attended a large consolidated school with a number of bigger boys who proceeded to lead me a "merry life." They had great fun in teasing and bullying the frightened preacher's kid who had so recently come to school! But for me, it was a miserable life, indeed.

I tell this story not because it is unique, for it is not, except in details. I tell it because every one of us, in his or her particular human situation, no matter how sheltered life might be for a time, sooner or later is dragged by the heels through hurtful and ego-threatening situations. Often these experiences leave scars and sometimes open wounds in our minds and hearts. Human life has a way of attacking our self-esteem and joyful confidence, reducing our inner status to less than zero.

What we do with these scars and wounds will determine to a great extent our wholeness and health, our peace and joy—or the lack of these essentials—for creative living with a sense of meaning and purpose. When these destructive experiences of youth are joined by the continuing hostility and injustice that sooner or later come to all, the necessity for a living faith becomes obvious. If this faith is to release the power of loving joy through adequate disciplines of the spirit, allowing us to find life something more than a sorry jest, a bad dream to be ended as soon as possible, it must grow. We must have what I am calling *Disciplines for Life*.

This book is being written out of my own life experiences and my observations of the value of a vital faith and the ways that it can bring adequate meaning and joyful purpose to our human lives in spite of all the draggings-by-our-heels we experience.

Before I go any further with my story, let me tell the story of another young man whose circumstances were just the opposite of mine. He was born to affluent parents in a large city, where he was given the best educational and social opportunities. He was popular among his peers, who shared his good times. At the age of twenty-one he possessed everything that most people think is necessary for life to the full. He was handsome and well dressed. He drove an expensive sports car and tasted every pleasure from promiscuous sex to alcohol and drugs. But each new high had to be higher than the last one. And each low was lower than the one before. Driven but empty, he tried vainly to fill the vacuum. One night, sick and hopeless, he mixed speed with sleeping pills, thinking the farce of his life would be over. Fortunately, his mother found him, unconscious but still alive. After being brought back to physical life and completing a stay in the hospital, he was put into a therapy group by his parents and doctor.

I met him as we sat together on a short plane trip many years later, and he told me his story. Clearly he was now a wealthy, successful businessman. Seeing the notes I was preparing for an address before a conference on evangelism, he observed, "You must be a reverend." I told him that I am a United Methodist bishop and that the notes were for an address I was to give to several hundred laypersons and pastors. I went on to speak of my concern for the lack of meaning and hope in so many people as indicated by the 400 percent increase in youth suicides.

He began to tell me his story. "I rarely talk with anyone on a plane, but since you are a Methodist bishop, I want you to know that I was brought up a Methodist. My parents took me to church and Sunday school. But when I was twenty-one, I tried to kill myself! I didn't succeed, and I was sent to a therapy group."

As he talked, he became almost feverish in his excitement. "Several in the group kept saying that if I wanted to kick the drug habit, I would have to accept Christ and have faith that he would help me. One day I burst out in pent-up anger. I stood up before them all and said, 'My problem isn't a God problem. I have believed in God and Christ since childhood. My problem is drugs.'"

"Was that your real problem?" I gently pushed him.

"Well, no, I guess my problem was lack of self-esteem. I hated myself. I had all and more of the things the world said I needed, yet I was empty and despondent, like the young boy in Houston we heard on TV. He said of his pal who had committed suicide, 'He didn't have any reason for living. Why shouldn't he kill himself?' I can identify with that."

In the brief time before the plane landed, my new acquaintance went on to tell me that his father, though a very good communicator in business and community affairs, had never really communicated his love for his son until recently, at the age of seventy-five. Before we parted at the airport, he took me by the hand and said earnestly, "Tell them tomorrow, these preachers and church leaders, tell them the one great word is *LOVE. Communicate love!"*

The real difference between my life at the age of twenty-one and this man's was not my poverty and the overt rejection by my peers, but the glorious fact that this love of which he spoke and that makes life infinitely worth living was communicated to me early and continuously by my mother and father. Their lives of devotion to the love of God in Christ opened the door for me to believe that I was loved by God, who, in Jesus, came very near to me even as a child. I can surely identify with this man who had come to a life worth living through his acceptance of the incredible love of God, which was made known to him by vital Christians he met after his attempted suicide. Until then, from what he saw in the lives of those around him professing to be Christians, he had never experienced such love as a reality.

There was one other point on which we could heartily agree: purely intellectual belief in God as revealed in Christ and superficial or even ardent church work and worship, as valuable as both may be, are not enough to fill life with joyful love and deep meaning.

I do not know any more of this man's story, but from what he shared with me in that brief conversation on the plane, I am confident that the meaninglessness and despair of his self-hatred were removed as the beliefs he had inherited became a firsthand experience of the love of God, making possible his own love for others, including his father. I also am confident that this was possible through a regularly and consciously disciplined life in which the eternal love became more and more a living reality. I know my own personal story in full, of course, and I believe it parallels in many ways the stories of others whom I know either personally or through reading accounts of their lives that have been made whole and significant by growth in mature faith. We all learned to accept and rejoice in practicing the disciplines that open the door for Life, spelled with a capital *L*. For this Life is God's most precious gift! In these pages, in an attempt to help others achieve this Life, I will utilize the personal account of my spiritual formation along with the testimony of others who, through the centuries, have found Christ the way to Life.

Jesus' central teachings declare and illustrate two ways to Life. In the paradoxical statement found in the Gospels of Matthew, Mark, and Luke, Jesus declares "Whoever wants to save his own life will lose it; but whoever loses his life for me and for the gospels will save it" (Mark 8:35, TEV). Jesus is saying at least these two truths about our lives: every human person wants life, longs for it, searches for it; and some find life, while others lose it. The difference is not in the longing and searching for life but in the *way* we search for it. Many seek life in the fulfillment of their own self-centered ideas of what is good, and thus lose the truly good life that is meant for all God's children. Only those who lose their narcissistic demands for life and are truly open and obedient to the highest good as revealed in Jesus and the continuing work of the Spirit in human life will find "life in all its fullness" (John 10:10, TEV). John 10:10, Mark 8:33-34, John 8:31 are only a few of the passages in which Jesus makes this way to the fullest life clear. "If anyone wants to come with me, . . . he must forget himself . . . and follow me" (Mark 8:34, TEV).

Here, in the beginning chapter of this book, let me affirm the unquestionable fact that I would not be alive today with anything resembling creativity, joy, and value in my life and work without having realized two things. The first of these is the agony and despair that results from undisciplined faith in the God of Christlike love. That is, I had possessed meanings and purposes for my life that I believed with the top of my mind and my conscious understanding but that had never been accepted and were often disobeyed by my deeper self. Like so many of my contemporaries who seek to live by a faith in someone or something bigger than they, I was a divided person. Part of me, most of the time, wanted to live by my ideals and convictions, while the deeper part of me rebelled. This split caused me to contradict and sometimes defy these convictions, bringing sorrow and disgust with myself.

For several years I could easily have joined W. Somer-
set Maugham, who said of himself, "There are times
when I look over the various parts of my character with
perplexity. I recognize that I am made up of several persons and that the person that at the moment has the upper hand will inevitably give place to another. But which
is the real one? All of them or none?" I earnestly wanted
to live by these fine ideals and values, but when the tests
of life came, I was often weak, shifting, and inadequate.
This was true of me as a person, a husband, a father, as
well as a minister-pastor-preacher in a Christian church.
Yes, I confess the truth about me.

> Within my earthly temple there's a crowd;
> There's one of us that's humble, one that's proud,
> There's one that's broken-hearted for his sins,
> There's one that unrepentant sits and grins;
> There's one that loves his neighbor as himself,
> And one that cares for naught but fame and pelf.
> From much corroding care I should be free
> If I could once determine which is me.[1]

I am painfully and wonderfully human—if you can
accept the paradox—and so are you. You too have phony
masks to remove. But, like me and anyone else who begins to find a life that is authentic and worth living in this
exciting but dangerous world, you will have to see your
masks, recognize them for what they are, and strip them
off. This was and is my first necessity for life, as it is
yours. This stripping off of our self-fabricated masks is
possible only as we lose ourselves in God's purpose.
Losing the false to find the true comes only to the one
who is increasingly sure of being infinitely loved by
God, as I shall illustrate and make plain.

The second thing I have come to realize about my life
has resulted in both a new insight into my true self and
the real world in which I live and the courageous ability
to live by these new-found insights. This has been a
costly experience indeed, similar to dying; for the old,
phony selves hate to die. But without this second realization, the realization of my splintered, divided self
would have destroyed my effectiveness, as it did for this

other young man, and left me in despair, as it has count-less thousands who simply cannot face the messes and musses caused by their own unworthy fears, hostilities, and feelings of inadequacy and pride. To this second re-alization I owe whatever creativity and aliveness there is in Lance Webb today. This book tells that story. I am de-scribing a priceless discovery: if I am to become the true Lance Webb that I believe the eternally creative and lov-ing Source and Ground of all life made me to be, I would have to take time to discipline my unconscious mind and spirit. I would be required by the very nature of my human life to take this time whether I thought I had it or not, whether I felt like it or not. I would have to do this through the regular, intelligent, faithful use of my con-scious mind in discovering who I am and what my re-sources are and in using the most priceless gift of human life, the great "I will," to be my authentic self in the service of others. All of this would be done in re-sponse to the Eternal Father-Mother Creator-Spirit who, I believe, is leading me to my life's fulfillment.

In my attempt to live by the faith in Christ I professed, I began to understand and practice these disciplines more thoroughly than I had previously ever understood as necessary. Until I saw the need for the disciplines of mind and spirit and until I had accepted and begun to practice them, I had been a sometimes free person but an oftentimes enslaved person. I was a struggler who lost as many battles as I won. I still don't win them all now, be sure of that. But on a January day in 1947, I de-cided my commitment of faith wasn't worth anything unless it was accompanied by a commitment to the dis-ciplines that would enable me to live that faith day by day. From that time I have lived increasingly on tiptoe. There have been moments, hours, and occasionally a day or several days when I neglected the disciplines and slipped back into the old futilities and conflicts. But even during recent years on the rack of arduous and urgent responsibilities, my life has become increasingly free and meaningful. I still have a long way to go, but I know the way and have traveled it for many years with more joy than I could ever have dreamed possible.

When I first began trying to live by a conscious faith, I was as sincere and dedicated a person as any mixed-up young man who had grown up with a lot of scars on his subconscious mind could be. I was fighting for the approval of my peers. When I left the one-teacher school where my father had taught me until I was thirteen, I had to learn to be a person in a rather frightening world. I was struggling to discover my true self and my mission, if I had one. Like a baby chicken, I was trying to pip the shell which hid me from freedom and life within and outside of me. I had to crawl out of my self-imposed lines of defense to see what this great, wide, wonderful world and its Creator had for me.

My first two years in college I spent seeking some identity as a reporter on the college newspaper and as solo trumpeter for the college band. Then, on Easter Sunday, 1928, I came to a realization that gave me a great spurt of personal growth in creativity and freedom. I was not in church that Sunday because I thought church was rather dull and I had other things to do. The Christian beliefs I had been taught as a child were in a state of suspension. That afternoon, as I tried to help my roommate meet a crisis in his life, I faced a sudden question— *what was my life for, anyway?* All at once I knew that the realities of the faith of my parents and others I had known would have to be reckoned with in addition to the realities of physics, chemistry, and the biological urges I felt so strongly.

That day I realized that only one thing would produce the peace and loving cooperation so desperately needed in my home, in my society, and in my country, which was in the beginning of the depression. The one thing needed most, I concluded, was the wholehearted conviction of faith that puts us in the frame of the family of God as revealed in Jesus Christ. This was my moment of decision to study for the Christian ministry and to do all I could to participate in a spiritual awakening. Even then I was convinced that this needed renewal of human life was coming. If it didn't, we would be in a mess. This realization was even before the atom bomb, World War II, the Korean and Vietnam wars, the pollution of our air and water, the great but threatening developments of high technology and nuclear energy.

For the next seventeen years, I struggled to get out of my selfish cocoon and grow into a mature person. I fought the battles of faith and doubt, of selfishness and self-giving, of love and hate. This battling went on all through college and graduate school and continued even as I tried to preach in little churches that my father and other trusting pastors provided. The struggle persisted as I went to my first assignment—the organizing and building of two new churches in Pampa, an oil-field town in west Texas. Here my high-flung, idealistic philosophy and theology were tried and found wanting, though the strong ardor of my struggle to proclaim the good news of the Christian faith did produce some results. After a year as chaplain of McMurry College, four years as pastor in Shamrock, and one year in Eastland, Texas, I was appointed to continue a newly begun ministry in University Park, Dallas. During these years I had a taste of what all young men and women experience when they go out, handicapped by a divided self, to win a worthy battle. I was completely committed, I thought, to being the best man I could be as the husband of a lovely wife and the father of three little girls, as a citizen of a good country, and as the pastor of a church that was growing so rapidly we were in a state of perpetual crisis.

Because I threw myself so completely into my life and work, I had some high moments of success and of personal victory over my inauthentic self. But I also had times when I almost gave up in despair. I would pray and read, seeking for help, and come out with a burst of new freedom and creativity. But after a few days, I would sink back into the same old rut of insecurity and into what occasionally would have to be called by its true names, envy and jealousy, as I compared myself with other ministers who had opportunities I thought I could handle as well or better than they. But here I was with this church and its challenging opportunities and harassing problems and needs. I loved the people and spent many hours ministering to them out of genuine concern, but one day in January, 1947, I had the shock of my life.

One of my good friends, a young attorney and lay leader in the church, sat down in my office and said to me, "Lance, we know you love us, but some of us wonder whether or not you are more concerned with getting this church built than with us!"

I knew there was some truth in his words. I was under a strong compulsion to build the much-needed church structure. My goal was good, but my obsessive demands were causing me to push too hard.

His words pierced my very soul. I could not get away from them as I sat a few days later in a meeting with other pastors and heard a very effective preacher talk about the necessity for "getting oneself off one's hands." That morning as I listened and as we closed the meeting, I made the second most momentous decision of my life. I had previously committed myself to follow Christ as best I understood him, but I had never committed myself to regular disciplines of prayer, reading, and thinking in the presence of God, nor had I been willing to submit myself to the discipline of a group with the same goal. I told my wife and my secretary that from that day on, the first thirty minutes or hour in my study every morning were to be given to the one purpose of meeting the truth of Christ and "getting my false self off my hands." However long it took, I was determined to find the resources and the insights I needed to fulfill my life and ministry. Nothing was to interfere other than an emergency in the life of one of my people or my own family.

Since that day, I have kept that commitment as faithfully as I have been able. From it and from other disciplines that will be described in this book have come a discovery of the most important things in my life today. Among these is the whole world of autobiographical literature containing the experiences of vital persons in every age. I spent six weeks the next summer in Union School of Theology, New York City, where I was privileged to take two courses with Dr. Douglas V. Steere, "The Devotional Life" and "The Biographies of the

Saints." Dr. Steere opened the door for me to resources I had not known existed. I found mirrored in the lives of vital Christians my own struggles and needs. I also saw the practical outworking of the deeper meanings of trust and love that Christ revealed. Here I met the undergirding challenge of the love of God that shone in Jesus Christ that was calling me to learn to love and trust others.

I discovered the means by which I could come through the low places when my feelings and misgivings were all running contrary to conscious faith. I received the power to come through what other Christians have called "the dark night of the soul," when outward circumstances and the cynical atheism of the world sought to throw me off the track.

The wonderful part is that the intervals between the low places of doubt and depression soon became much farther apart as they were met with renewed faith and greater insights. I knew with Paul that "when I am weak, then I am strong" (2 Cor. 12:10, TEV). I began what has been one of the most helpful disciplines in my entire life. In a book with a blank page for every day in the year, I wrote down selections from scripture, the experiences of some other seeker after truth, a poem, the verse of a hymn, or the honest description of what was taking place within me. Generally, I would read until I came upon a sentence or a paragraph that really spoke to me. I recorded the selection in my own poor handwriting (which most people can't read), and then I wrote my appropriate response. Sometimes it was a confession. At other times it was insight into why I failed and decision as to what I should do about the situation I was facing. Often it was to write my new commitment, my new trust, and my thanksgiving and praise for the One in whose presence I can truthfully say, "I have strength for anything through him who gives me power" (Phil. 4:13, NEB).

These books—one for each year since then—reflect the story of my pilgrimage through the difficult testings and opportunities that have come to me: the weary burdens I have borne, the triumphant experiences of victory over the demands of my phony self, the equally precious experience of sharing with others who were winning the victory of faith. I can turn back through these books and trace the crises by which my faith has grown and the divisions and conflicts within my subconscious mind that have been increasingly overcome.

If a fire were to start in my home, the first thing I would seek to save would be these "Living the Faith" notebooks. They are precious to me for what they represent—the way in which the Holy Spirit of Christ-like love has led me, fighting and kicking much of the time, out of my little self and into a life that is freer and more creative than I ever dreamed it could be.

Behind the pages that follow is this experience that I have shared in bare outline. I have not won all the battles. I still doubt at times, but I believe with infinitely greater assurance than ever that, as Jesus promised the woman at the well (John 4:7-15), there is a well of grace springing up into life eternal at the center of my now and of my future as well. I believe there is nothing more wonderful than having buckets with which to draw from this deep well of life and having the readiness to use these buckets regularly and thankfully. Life's greatest joys come when, caringly, lovingly, I am able to help some of my brothers and sisters in God's great family to drink and eat and live!

I write this with neither the expectancy nor the desire that you will try to follow exactly the same approaches I have. I know this is impossible, for each of us is wonderfully, though peculiarly, made. I do earnestly hope, however, that these experiences and insights may do for you what others have done for me—point to the Well of Life and help you to find and use the buckets!

2

Buckets for the Well of Life

We are all insatiably thirsty for the living water that flows from the Well of Life. The story of Jesus and the Samaritan woman at the well is an apt parable of our avid thirst for Life and the need for the spiritual disciplines that make it possible. Of course, we long for physical life at its best—witness the multiplicity of health clubs and the millions of people who discipline themselves by jogging and in diet. Health foods are used by an increasing number of those who seek to avoid the dangers of cardiovascular diseases. A far deeper hunger, however, exists for the inner joys and satisfactions of life on tiptoe with meaning and purpose that lasts even when physical health is going or gone.

When Jesus asked the woman at the well for a drink, "the Samaritan woman said, 'What! You, a Jew, ask drink of me, a Samaritan woman?'

"Jesus answered her, 'If only you knew what God gives, and who it is that is asking you for a drink, you would have asked him and he would have given you living water'" (John 4:9–10, NEB).

Jesus' answer describes the great promise of Life to the full which his life illustrates. "'Everyone who drinks this water will be thirsty again, but whoever drinks the water that I shall give him will never suffer thirst any more. The water that I shall give him will be an inner spring always welling up for eternal life.'

"'Sir,' said the woman, 'give me that water, and then I shall not be thirsty'" (John 4:14–15, NEB).

Our primary human question, whether or not we recognize it, is: *How do we find the inner springs welling up for eternal life now and for the future?* The Samaritan woman's first response to Jesus' promise was to cry in unbelief, "Sir, you have no bucket and the well is deep!" This response underlines our second necessary question: *The well is so deep. Where shall we find the buckets with which to draw living water?* Some lines from William Cowper describe our human predicament:

> [Deliver us] from the toil
> Of dropping buckets into empty wells,
> And growing old in drawing nothing up![1]

So many of us have no buckets, and the well is deep! We know in our best moments that there is, or ought to be, a well of living water. From this precious water we may drink and never thirst. But the wells so many find readily available are empty or filled with poisoned water. And for the well of living water, we have no buckets with which to draw. If only we could be saved from the futility and toil of dropping our buckets into these empty or poisoned wells and growing old drawing nothing up. For some, suicide seems a better, though tragic, choice. For others, an existence of boredom and emptiness is all that seems possible.

Why this lack of living water? Jesus answers in one of his "hard sayings": "The gate is wide and the way is easy that leads to destruction, and those who enter by it are many. For the gate is narrow and the way is hard, that leads to life, and those who find it are few" (Matt. 7:13, RSV). The empty buckets symbolize the lack of adequate disciplines—the wide and easy way that leads to the loss of life to the full.

The stories of myself and the other young man in the first chapter of this book also illustrate this point. Both of us were losing our ability to live with joyful, loving purpose. This had nothing to do with the presence or absence of affluence or social and emotional adjustments in our human situation. We were losing our true lives because we were not disciplined in living out our belief in the love of God poured out upon us in so many ways. We were believers from the top of our minds but unbelievers from the bottom of our hearts. We did not believe in the center of the unconscious mind or the conscious. The affluent young man's mental acquiescence to the faith of his parents and his church was not adequate to prevent him from seeking to destroy himself. My mental acquiescence to the faith in Christ taught by my parents, in spite of their loving teachings and affirmation, did not prevent me from the self-hatred that was threatening my powers for free and creative living. Neither of us was to be saved by "God talk." We had had plenty of that. We were to be saved by a new and wondrous awareness of the presence of the living Christ who loved us as we were and could become. This was the deep well from which we were to draw living water!

Let's return again to our primary question: How may we be made aware of and accept this priceless love, which, like the rays of the sun, whether recognized or not, is continually beating upon us?

What are the buckets (disciplines) by which we draw the living water of Christlike love so that we may be able to love even as we are loved? How may we receive love that blesses rather than curses, that frees rather than enslaves, liberates rather than imprisons; joy that is independent of external circumstances; peace, the shalom of wholeness and health, that enables us to do the best things in the worst times?

The buckets can be identified as the "Means of Grace," which John Wesley described in one of his most significant sermons.[3] Wesley discussed the ways or means of God's grace by which we are spiritually formed in Christ. The apostle Paul touched on the same idea when he repeatedly described his task as "fully proclaiming [Christ's] message . . . to make known [God's] . . . rich and glorious secret . . . that Christ is in you, which means that you will share in the glory of God. . . . We warn and teach . . . in order to bring each one into God's presence as a mature individual in union with Christ" (Col. 1:25–28, TEV). To the Galatians, Paul wrote this simple yet profound statement of supreme mission describing his love: "My dear children! Once again, just like a mother in childbirth, I feel the same kind of pain for you until Christ's nature is formed in you" (Gal. 4:19, TEV).

The whole process of using disciplines by which, according to Maxie Dunnam, "we are alive in Christ," is called, by both Protestants and Catholics, "spiritual formation." In his inspiring book, *Alive in Christ*, Dr. Dunnam gives the clearest definition of spiritual formation in Christ that I have heard: "*Spiritual formation* is that dynamic process of receiving through faith and appropriating through commitment, discipline, and action, the living Christ into our own life to the end that our life will conform to, and manifest the reality of Christ's presence in the world."[3]

Here, in Dr. Dunnam's last seven words, is the catch: *Is the presence of the living Christ a reality in this world?* Do we really believe that God in Christ is or can be the motivating factor in our lives? Indeed, this is the "Catch-22" for us and our world.

I was startled recently by the reprint of an article by Dr. Harry Emerson Fosdick, originally published in *The Christian Century* in 1919, warning that, with all the idealism following World War I, "our modern world is headed straight for some gigantic disappointments. . . . It takes far more brotherly spirit to run a League of Nations than to run a village; . . . the Christian faith in God must grow accordingly." What a realistic prophecy! Over these sixty-five years we have had only more war, starvation, crime, terror, and nuclear confrontation! Why has our faith not grown adequately? Fosdick answers:

> The sense of God's [love as a] reality is a different experience from the belief that God exists. . . . *Atheism is not our greatest danger, but a shadowy sense of God's reality.* We do not disbelieve that God exists, but we often lack a penetrating and convincing consciousness that we are dealing with him and he with us. *This is the inner problem of prayer.*

He concludes that our single most important understanding, if we are to have a life of peace and justice, is
that *"a vital consciousness of the divine presence shall make
glory at the center."*[4]

Life with glory at the center! Life infinitely, magnifi-
cently worth living! *Eternal life "in Christ" through the
God of love in Christ as a priceless reality!*

An inscription I found pinned on the door of the student senate office in one of our universities had this
quote from D. H. Lawrence: "Heaven knows what we
mean by Reality: telephones, tinned meat, Charlie
Chaplin, water taps and world salvation, presumably!" I
don't know about telephones and water taps, but I believe the highest reality is concerned with personal and
world salvation—salvation from the fears, hates, greeds,
and terrors of man's inhumanity to the love that sets us
free to life that is full and vital. Any other kind of freedom is empty!

Dag Hammarskjöld, the great Swedish statesman
and secretary general of the United Nations, believed
that the man of Galilee best sums up the mighty truth
that describes the awesome power ruling our universe.
He was one of the thousands whose lives have been
made meaningful and creative by their belief that
through Jesus Christ comes the gift of meaning and
hope for themselves and for humanity. Writing in his diary on Christmas Eve, 1960, one year and a half before
his tragic death in Africa, Hammarskjöld declared the
faith to which his life was joined: "How proper it is that
Christmas should follow Advent.—For him who looks
towards the future, the Manger is situated on Golgotha,
and the Cross has already been raised in Bethlehem."[5]

Gustaf Aulén, commenting on Dag Hammarskjöld's
faith, says that for Hammarskjöld "the whole life-
achievement of Jesus is to be seen as an incarnation of
the love of God—of God in man." And I would add the
love of people for other people because of this love of
God. Hammarskjöld's life motto was in the last lines of
an old Swedish hymn: "There is nothing that is not won
by the love which suffers."[6]

Is it true that the mightiest force on earth is the invincible power of the Spirit that was in Jesus and in the strong, humble, loving life to which he calls? Is it true that nothing is ever won but by the love that suffers?

I have believed this most of my life, and with conscious, understanding commitment since I was eighteen, but there have been moments of doubt. After making my decision in college to study for the Christian ministry because of this new-found faith, I found myself faced with the convictions of intelligent people such as Henry Nelson Wieman, John Dewey, and others who claimed that the only God there is must be something like the group equivalent of Santa Claus or the sum total of values most important to humankind! They believed that prayer at its best is autosuggestion and self-hypnotism, or just good positive thinking! This humanistic picture of humanity who, despite its longing for a loving Creator, must go it alone, left me in a major crisis. My emotional and mental stability was threatened, as well as my chosen ministry. The way I was delivered from this crisis of faith in my life is described in a later chapter. Here it is enough merely to say that I decided to cast my lot with those whose faith in God as revealed and interpreted in Jesus enabled them to make such large contributions to their own times and to the betterment of humankind.

That act of faith brought me to a fresh burst of courage and hope and corresponding creativity. My personality and effectiveness grew and life was full. I have, however, continued to have doubts as I have seen again and again unscrupulous persons taking advantage of kind and loving people and as I have endured the horrors of living through World War II and other tragic events in these last fifty years. At times I have rebelled until being given some fresh revealing of the deepest truth of life— that nothing is ever won but by the love that suffers, for "love is of God and God is love." I agree with Dostoyevsky that "my hosannas have gone through whirlwinds of doubt." Doubtless Dag Hammarskjöld and every other man or woman of faith would say the same thing. For surely one who has never doubted has never truly believed.

How can I be certain? This question points up the crises of faith in this age of assurance and belief in the scientific world and of doubt and frustration in the personal and social world. It is here that the ability to love and give oneself for others is often lacking and yet so necessary. The fact that so many are *unsure* or simply *do not believe* the basic assumption that strong, wise love is at the heart of things is both our first problem and our greatest tragedy. How can we be interested in God's will and purpose for our lives unless there is at least this minimum conviction upon which we are willing to live and die? How else can we answer the following questions: Does might make right? Do hatred and selfishness really pay in the long run? Is sacrificial, self-giving love really foolish, or is it "God's way of righting wrong" (Rom. 1:17, NEB)?

Some may believe that the answer to these questions is simply their own choice, the opposite perhaps being just as true for someone else. Some may believe that love may be true for St. Francis and Albert Schweitzer, but whether or not they choose to give themselves out of such love matters only to them. But, if there is no truth common to us all, how could there be any respect for laws based on "common good" when there is no common good? We know the necessity of protecting the well-being of others from the freedom of the few to do as they please. Clearly, the morality upon which our human health and existence depend rests upon our faith or unfaith in the highest understanding of God we know. *Is or is not Christlike, caring love the mightiest force ruling our human lives?* Ivan, a character in Dostoyevsky's *The Brothers Karamazov,* rationalized, "Since there is no God and no devil, then everything is permissible," and proceeded to justify the murder of his father. If anything goes, why be concerned about injustice in Africa, Central America, Afghanistan, in our own cities or even in our families? Why respect the value of persons if man is nothing but a "forked radish" with no destiny beyond a dusty death, or, as Ernest Haeckel puts it, "a vertical vertebra with a perfect sewage system"?

How can we be sure enough of the truth of God's love to discover and sing the new song for our new age in spite of the cacophony of noisy contradictions? In responding to these questions, it seems to me that there are four things required of each of us:

First, we must be *convinced* of the reality of God as seen most clearly in the spirit, life, death, and victory of Jesus Christ.

Second, we must be *reconciled* to the loving purposes of this mighty Spirit who rules the universe but gives us freedom to fight and reject ourselves and our true destiny.

Third, we must be *committed* without reservation to live our lives in line with those purposes as we are able to discover and understand them.

Fourth, we must be voluntarily *disciplined* by continued acts of faith to use and perform the means that best enable us to live and die by this faith.

Spiritual formation "in Christ" includes all four of these requirements. A living faith can be achieved through the continual, regular use of the disciplines for life as I shall seek to describe and illustrate them in the following chapters.

To sum up, the basic assumption of my faith is that there are streams of living water into which we may place our human roots to draw the grace and strength to live and act with nobility, dignity, courage, and wise, strong love. The putting down of these roots is the most important action of which the human mind and spirit are capable. The act of putting down these roots—the use of these buckets—is what Christians have meant by these old words: prayer, worship, contemplation, recollection, and meditation. The words describe the old pieties that have been abandoned by so many people who still cling wistfully to their belief that God is in Christ.

This book will seek to dig beneath the old words and the old pieties to find the new song of Life we are all longing to sing, and to help us sing it with enthusiasm and joy, with great courage and hope. Only as we translate our intellectual beliefs into this kind of creative, life-bringing action of faith, made possible by meaningful disciplines, will we ever stand up and begin to live in peace and love, "turned on to joy"! When this happens, we really will have something to sing about! The well of living water within us is overflowing when we are glad to use our buckets!

Part Two

HOW TO UNDERSTAND
AND
USE THE DISCIPLINES

3

The Basic Disciplines of
True Perspectives

Disciplines of any kind are never easy. Disciplines for their own sake are never likely to be enjoyed. One accepts and follows through on them only as one sees and desires the results above all else. It is easy to dream of becoming a famous musician or of winning the decathlon in the Olympics, of being a successful author, business or professional person—doctor, lawyer, teacher, minister, diplomat. But between the dream and the realization are endless hours of discipline and hard work.

"Practice, practice, practice! That's my secret!" Paderewski's oft-quoted statement is true in any area of human life. He said in effect, "If I miss practicing one day, I know it. If I miss one week, my wife knows it. If I miss two weeks, my audience knows it!"

"Discipline is an absolute necessity for the Christian life," wrote Dr. Maxie Dunnam in his very practical and useful *Workbook on Spiritual Disciplines.* "We may be converted to Christ in the miracle of a moment, but becoming a saint [a mature person in Christ] is the task of a lifetime."[1] The bucket of living water drawn from the deep well of life is not enough to last longer than an hour or a day at most! We must continually draw up the water—or, to change the figure, keep the channels open so the streams of living water may flow from the depths of our consciousness in Christ in us. "A vital consciousness of the divine presence [that] shall make glory at the center" is never an accident, something suddenly imposed on us by God that we will never lose. It is, rather, through the "Practice of the Presence," as Brother Law-rence describes it, that we find an increasing power to live in loving joy and peace with God's ineffable glory in and through us.

For this reason, Richard J. Foster speaks of "The Cele-bration of Discipline" as the door to liberation that frees us from the false and twisted values and attitudes of our self-centered and culture-centered prison.[2] The disci-plines for life are not practiced with gritted teeth and furrowed brow, but with relaxed gladness, as Psalm 16:11 declares, "In thy presence is fulness of joy" (KJV).

Sometimes it is true that we must begin the practice of a spiritual discipline in agony, prompted by our empty feelings of alienation and futility, as by an act of faith we dare to drop our spiritual buckets into Christ's promises of living water. Certainly, there are times when we do not feel like doing it; but as we proceed by continued acts of trust, the disciplines become the door to emanci-pation from the tyrannies of our pettiness, self-pity, loneliness, resentment, and the self-centered demands that imprison us.

"What makes life splendid is the constant awareness of God," Dr. Albert Edward Day writes in his classic book, *Discipline and Discovery,* used since 1947 as the Manual for the Disciplined Order of Christ.

> God is not real to most of us because of the condition of our consciousness. He is closer to our minds every moment than our own thoughts. He is nearer to our hearts than our own feelings. He is more intimate with our wills than our most vigorous decisions. If we are not aware of him, it is not because he is not with us. It is, in part, because our consciousness is so under the sway of other interests that it cannot turn to him with the lov-ing attention which might soon discern him.[3]

The problem with most professing Christians is that they have never been taught that an intellectual accep-tance of the reality of God in Christ must be translated into living, growing, experience of who God is and who we are as we encounter God in maturing faith. This is indeed the tragedy of the church over the ages. The tragedy began in the early church as Paul described those "who preserve the outward form of religion but are a standing denial of its reality" (2 Tim. 3:5, NEB). The Revised Standard Version translates this passage, "holding the form of religion but denying the power."

The story of Constantine is typical of what has happened over the centuries. Constantine's mother was a devout Christian. Her son was not interested in Christianity and resisted her religious entreaties until just before the crucial battle with Maxentius, which would decide who was to be emperor. In his dreams, Constantine saw a flaming cross with the words, "In this sign thou shalt conquer." He awoke and, on his knees, promised that if he won the battle he would become a Christian. He adopted the cross as the sign on his banners, won the battle, and was baptized as a Christian along with thousands of his followers. This was one of the saddest days in the history of the church, according to some church historians. For, though Christians were no longer persecuted and Christianity became the popular religion, there was lacking any effective spiritual formation in Christ. No one taught Constantine and the multitude of new Christians the true meaning of the cross or how to pray and worship, live and act in the spirit of Christ. "If any man have not the Spirit of Christ, he is none of his" (Rom. 8:9, KJV).

In every age the story has been repeated: as the "Christian Phalangists" massacred a thousand Palestinian civilians—mostly the aged and children in a refugee camp in Beirut—television cameras zoomed in on the soldiers wearing crosses on their uniforms! The IRA in Ireland commits similar atrocities in the name of Christ! And in America, millions have joined churches professing to believe in Christ but never being spiritually formed "in the mind of Christ." No wonder the world today is filled with such evils as hunger, unemployment, crime, and terror! Millions of professing Christians do not know and share the love of Christ, because they do not know from experience the mind of Christ. Why? For the simple reason that their sincere mental assent to belief that Christ reveals the love of God was never transformed into an experience of that love. Their conscious thought and attention was never focused on the living reality of the transforming presence seen in Jesus and in those whose lives incarnate that infinite love.

It is strange that this kind of undisciplined belief should exist in the spiritual realm, where our awareness or lack of awareness of God either enables us to live our lives eagerly, on tiptoe with loving joy, or blocks us with a sense of futility and meaninglessness that makes life not worth living. Something is missing in so many "Christians"! We *know* so much more than we *do*. There is a tragic gap between our scientific and technical knowledge and our human ability to perceive the crucial moral and spiritual insights needed for creative action.

The Necessity for Disciplines of the Mind and Spirit

The priceless perspectives we crave can come only through a deeper insight into "grace and reality," and "grace and reality are ours through Jesus Christ" (John 1:17, MOFFATT). It is true that many professing Christians would agree with this in principle, but unfortunately their lives remain unaffected. There is nothing attractive or helpful in their lives to convince and guide others. Why? Largely because most of us Christians are undisciplined.

Clearly all the tremendous developments of science have come about through intensive and dedicated disciplines on the part of individuals and groups. Think of Jonas Salk and his quest for the vaccine that would prevent polio—the hours and days, the months and years of preparation, of testing, retesting, failing, and trying again and again. So with the groups of researchers in NASA, seeking to develop the conditions in spacesuits and ships that would make travelers to the moon or in space shuttles safe and comfortable. Tens of thousands of hours and days spent by many thousand scientists, engineers, astronauts, all coordinated to the goal of landing on the moon—all of this patient and persistent discipline was required for a successful moon landing.

Just as the disciplines of science have given us insight into the requirements or laws of the physical universe, so the spiritual disciplines are the oft forgotten or denied requirements for perspectives in our personal and social lives. This perspective will provide us with the needed insights into the "grace and truth" that came supremely in Jesus Christ and are reflected in the great procession of his followers in every age. The disciplines are the connecting links or roots by which such priceless perspectives come.

Look for a moment at the meaning of this word *discipline*. The dictionary defines it as "training that develops self-control, character, orderliness, and efficiency . . . acceptance of or submission to authority and control." But submission to whose authority? Whose control? That is the primary question. Is it the authority that begins and ends in my own little god-self with all the dozen conflicting ego demands striving for mastery? Is it the authority of conformism to whatever little gods I accept from my peer group or the customs of my community that may temporarily give meaning and prop up my sagging self-confidence? Or is it the authority of the Lord of life with the way and the truth—the Spirit I meet in Christ through the human Jesus and in my own deepest insights—that I believe is in the very nature of things?

The authority that makes disciplines acceptable must be from *within* us, for to be effective, disciplines must be self-imposed. They must be voluntarily chosen rather than externally enforced. Self-imposed disciplines result in freedom, but a discipline imposed from the outside results in slavery. By our very nature we tend to rebel against such external impositions.

For instance, we are seeing a rebellion in our time against the rigid sex ethics imposed by puritanical customs. This rebellion, in the form of sexual permissiveness, has become so repulsive and binding to many that some people are beginning to react against it and the pendulum is swinging back toward what may be a more responsible approach to sex. It is indeed against our very nature to accept enforced slavery to anything, whether it is the rigid demands of current mores in our society, the commands of a domineering father, the requirements of a totalitarian state, or the demands of a stern and unbending God of wrath and judgment. "The fear of the Lord is the beginning of wisdom" (Psalm 111:10, RSV), says the ancient biblical proverb, but this fear is compounded of awe, respect, and a response to the self-giving love that in the Old Testament left the Israelites singing, "Thou art good and doest good; teach me thy statutes" (Psalm 119:68, RSV).

In this chapter we are to consider the deep roots, the connecting links between our *little human perspectives* and the *eternally true perspectives of Jesus Christ.* These roots are grown or developed by the disciplines we accept voluntarily and wholeheartedly.

The failure to see from true perspectives is the root cause of much of our human misery and despair, as it has been in all ages. We, like the people of Judah, have forgotten the truth Jeremiah tried unsuccessfully to teach. "Turn back, every one of you, from his evil course; mend your ways and your doings. But they answer, 'Things are past hope. We will do as we like, and each of us will follow the promptings of his own wicked and stubborn heart'" (Jer. 18:11–13, NEB). The people of Judah refused to listen to him. Judah did fall, and when Jerusalem was destroyed in 586 B.C., most of Jeremiah's people were taken in exile to Babylon.

Undisciplined excesses in food, sex, alcohol, and material things—to which we have added drugs, movies, and TV—and unbridled hatred and defiance of each other can but lead to a destruction so total it is unthinkable! The current generation describes the mind of this age in a way strangely similar to Jeremiah's description of his people twenty-five hundred years ago in their time of futility and despair.

Millions today would justify their attitudes and actions in words something like this: Things are really past hope. There is nothing we can do to change the evils about us, including scars on our subconscious minds left by our parents, grandparents, and the chains of the establishment—government, education, church, culture. Yes, things are past hope, for hope is itself a liar.

Memory is unbearable because in both hope and memory there is a "no exit road" called "death." So I will live only in the here and now. I will live with innocence, spontaneity, novelty—all the pleasure I can summon. I will forget the past and ignore the future!

Obviously, we are responding to our feelings of insignificance, powerlessness, and meaninglessness in the personal and social realm, just as the people of ancient Judah were. They too were surrounded by enemies—Babylonians, Chaldeans, and Egyptians. Now the enemies are called the depressed or inflated economy, the military and industrial establishments, the health of our loved ones or of ourselves, or the Communists! Now, as then, there is no escape from our own finitude and frailty.

Jeremiah's answer to his people's futilities was sharp and to the point: They followed the promptings of wicked and stubborn hearts. I'm sure they didn't appreciate this incisive diagnosis any more than we do. Do we really think our hearts are wicked and stubborn? No, it's the president, or the police, or the system, or the hierarchy, or the Communists, or the people over thirty, or under thirty, or the racists, or the wife, or the husband—not me!

What we need is a good view of this "heart" or "subconscious mind," which depth psychology can help us see if we are not afraid to look. When we do look, we begin to recognize that indeed "the heart is deceitful and sick, who can fathom it?" (Jer. 17:9, AUTHOR PARAPHRASE). The old translations use the word *wicked* here. Both words include rationalizations, false motivations, and unrecognized desires and values that are the hidden blocks in the channels of the water of life, cutting off the roots, so that we too have "rejected the fountain of living water" (Jer. 17:13, NEB).

The diagnosis is contemporary indeed. Consider this passage from psychiatrist Carl Jung's *Modern Man in Search of a Soul,* as he describes our human sickness:

> We have built a monumental world about us, and we have slaved for it with unequalled energy . . . and what we find

when we look within must necessarily be as it is, shabby and insufficient.[4]

From his *Psychology and Alchemy* come these even more significant words describing our inner sickness:

> The great events of our world as planned and executed by man do not breathe the spirit of Christianity but rather of unadorned paganism. These things originate in a psychic condition that has remained archaic and has not been even remotely touched by Christianity. . . . Christian civilization has proved hollow to a terrifying degree; it is . . . veneer, but the inner man has remained untouched and therefore unchanged. *His soul is out of key with his external beliefs; in his soul the Christian has not kept pace with external developments. . . . Christ only meets them from without, never from within the soul; that is why dark paganism still reigns there.*[5]

The Destruction of Inner Paganism

Our first and greatest need is perspective—insight—clear vision into ourselves as well as beyond ourselves to the reality behind all realities, which we call God. Therefore *these roots, or channels, by which such perspectives come, must be dug out, cut through, and opened up to let the true meaning, value, and power of life through. If our inner life is pagan, unchanged by our Christian or other good beliefs, it is not surprising that we do not live and act by them and that we are still in the heathen age of morality so wholly inadequate for the age of space travel and nuclear threats!*

Of course this is not the picture of human life as painted by those who glory in the freedom and grandeur of scientific man. Yet the tragic fact of human life with all our scientific know-how is that secular man has the power to make fruitful everything in the universe but himself. Through science and technology we have power to bring untold energy from the atom, oil from the earth, abundant harvest from the desert, food from the ocean, power from the sun, power for everything except to bring life to ourselves and humankind.

Yet even this power is awaiting us as a gift. But this gift

is given only to those who trust themselves to something more than other men. It is for those who are open and willing to trust and be obedient in love to the eternal God. We recognize this truth immediately in the physical world as well as in the world of music and the arts. Handel, after hearing his *Messiah* played for the first time, cried exuberantly and gratefully, "It was not from me; it was from above." Albert Einstein, when asked how he came by the theory of relativity, replied in utter humility, "It was given me. . . . He who does not pause to wonder or stand wrapt in awe is as good as dead. There is no life in him." The true scientist, according to Aldous Huxley, is one who is willing to sit down before the facts like a little child.

How strange that secular man has done this in every part of life except in the interior life from which all meaning, hope, joy, peace, and love come. Instead, this inner life, as Jung puts it, remains full of "dark paganism" where the demons of hate, fear, greed, prejudice, and selfishness still reign.

What Cannot Human Beings Do?

The woman at the well of Jacob in Samaria found the answer that the modern world, with all its sophisticated scientific knowledge, is only beginning to discover. The woman understood her own deepest question and its answer. *What cannot a man or a woman do? They cannot by themselves draw water from the Well of Life, for they have no bucket with which to draw and the well is deep.* But water is there, as Jesus promised her. All who drink the water of physical, material accomplishment will thirst again, but whoever drinks the water Christ gives will never thirst. Instead there will be a spring of water welling up, bubbling over with eternal life. And by *eternal life*, Jesus clearly did not mean only a life after death, but life that is eternal in quality and meaning *now*.

The ones who are truly human, as pointed out in chapter 2, have found the bucket to draw this living water and use it regularly, whether in the age of science or in the pre-Copernican age. They are the ones who have learned to let their roots go deep down within their own lives and cultures to the springs of living water!

We need to hear again the warnings of Jeremiah as well as Jung. "A curse on the man who trusts in man and leans for support [only] on human kind, while his heart is far from the Lord! He shall be like a juniper in the desert; when good comes he shall not see it" (Jer. 17:5–6, NEB). What a universal description of the human experience. Trusting only in oneself and others, one cannot see the good in self-giving, suffering love, in self-sacrificial cooperation with neighbors that alone brings true peace and full, joyous life. Secular people in their search for the goods of life miss the true good. For example, many parents who found difficult times making a living during the depression determined that their children would not have to struggle so much for their material needs. They have lavished these "things" on their children only to find that these children are often unappreciative and are lacking in the true values of life that their parents had no time to share!

To summarize this cogent parable of life, let me paraphrase these words of Jeremiah.

> Deep rooted is the life who trusts in God—
> The living Reality in whom one lives, moves, and has
>   one's being.
> The individual of faith is not famished and starving
>   in a salt land where no one can live.
> That person carries water through deep roots from the
>   streams of grace which never run dry.

What are the spiritual roots which humanity, with all its science, still needs to let grow deep down into the springs of living water? One thing clear from the beautiful symbolism that is found so many places in the Old and New Testaments is that this water is found not in isolation, but in a free fellowship with others.

The water is the grace of God—the word *grace* meaning the undeserved, unearned gift of the gracious Creator. The Judeo-Christian faith declares that the spirit of insight, wisdom, love, and compassion is the very presence of the Holy Spirit, Immanuel, "God with us."

The springs of living water are the springs of *perspective* which give understanding and insight into the reality that is really valuable and eternally good. The *roots* by which these springs are reached are the roots of our conscious and unconscious human relationships with the eternal Giver of Life whom Jesus called Father. Through God and the beloved son Jesus Christ, we are able to enter into a loving relationship with our fellow humans as we all share in the spirit and drink of the living water that flows so freely.

The roots may be described by old familiar words: worship, prayer, communion, meditation, adoration, confession, petition, intercession, thanksgiving, commitment, obedience, service, giving, and acting in God's name. But these words need to be reinterpreted today because, for many people, they are dead and meaningless. Nevertheless, they represent a primary necessity for every person, and if we stop using them and the methods they signify, we will have to get some new words and new methods that will have the same effect. "[Vital] religion is not primarily a set of suppositions to be believed or disbelieved, but a set of skills that one employs in living. Such skills are acquired by learning the stories of Israel and Jesus well enough not only to interpret the world, but to do so in specifically Christian terms."[6]

These skills will be ways in which we open our own consciousness so that, instead of being embarrassed by God's presence, we will be inspired and empowered for life.

For, to summarize our human situation, there is no living water of loving, trusting relationships without roots that go deep into our relationship with our Creator Spirit and with those who through the centuries have known this relationship. There are no roots without conscious intent, that is, conscious willingness to discipline ourselves regularly in the use of our intelligence as we seek to learn from those who have gone before and willingness to practice the acceptance of ourselves in the presence of this Christ Spirit in whom we live and have our very being. From such living relationships come the

insights and perspectives without which we find ourselves "dwelling among rocks in the wilderness, in a salt
land where no man can live!"

Our Predicament

Our predicament is here presented in two parts. First,
we dislike discipline, defined as steady, regular, consis-
tent, continuous attention in practice by thought,
words, and acts. The word itself has an offensive sound,
especially to a permissive generation. For we want to do
as we like when we like, following the promptings of our
deceitful, evil, and stubborn hearts. "All we like sheep
have gone astray," wrote the prophet Isaiah, "We have
turned every one to his own way" (Isa. 53:6, RSV). And
as the psalmist told us, "You hate discipline" (Psalm
50:17, RSV).

Remember the parable of the one sheep who, being
smarter than the rest, despised them as "sheepish" in
following the shepherd. The one sheep knew where the
green grass was without the help of any shepherd. It left
and for a while it enjoyed its freedom. The grass was
green and the sheep was proud of itself. Soon, however,
the grass gave way to a thicket with brambles in which
the sheep was lost. The thorns pierced its wool and it
became hungry and cold. It could no longer see either its
fellow sheep or the shepherd. Suddenly, it looked
around and saw the wolf coming. The sheep turned in
fear and started running as fast as it could, but the wolf
was gaining on it, nipping at its heels. Then it found itself on the edge of a precipice. It had two choices: to
jump over the precipice or to turn and face the wolf. This
sheep did what many human sheep never do. It turned
and faced the wolf. When it did, to its amazement it
found that there was not a wolf at all, but the shepherd's
dog sent to bring it back to the green pastures!

This story represents our human dislike to be led and
guided. It also depicts the tragedy that comes to so
many who insist on always "doing their own thing." I
have used this story with numerous counselees—
alcoholics, marital sufferers, rebellious children and

youth. Its value depends on how much confidence the one who goes one's own way comes to have in the Good Shepherd. The discipline of following even God requires a conviction and a commitment of trusting faith.

The second part of our predicament is that the words to describe the needed disciplines (or roots) of life are old words encrusted with wrong attitudes and approaches. Together they form what has been called *Christian piety,* and piety is not a very desirable word even to talk about, much less to accept and practice. (Who wants to be pious?) Piety has, like these other words such as *prayer, worship,* and *obedience,* been associated with many false approaches to life and its meaning.

Of course, there are many different kinds of piety: Christian, Moslem, Hindu, secular, and others. There are also many kinds of Christian piety: Puritan, Victorian, Methodist, Amish, Roman Catholic, Lutheran, and so forth. Social action piety for some is all the rage. If you are opposed to war and to racism, then adultery, drunkenness, and even dope addiction are acceptable, or at least tolerated. This is the opposite, of course, of the piety of the average Christian who may not be too concerned with war or racism, but is horrified at sexual deviations or by what a person drinks or smokes. In addition, there is the piety of a moralism based on certain absolute principles (from the Bible or from the culture around us). As James Whitcomb Riley described it, "The meanest man I ever saw allus kep' inside o' the law!" There is the rather generalized Christian piety of religious duties—go to church, pay your part of its upkeep, say your prayers, and read a few verses from the Bible at the breakfast table or before going to bed at night. There is also a hedonistic form of piety which agrees with Ernest Hemingway, "Anything that's pleasurable is good; anything that's painful is bad."

Now, since it is so easy to misunderstand the authentic meaning of *piety,* why use the word at all? For the simple reason that it is a meaningful word if we use it to describe the pattern or style of being and doing that which we have chosen because of our own particular interpretation of faith; that is, our piety is the style of life, the things we do or don't do, that results from what we really believe is ultimate or, at least, most important.

Whether or not the disciplines for life recommended and described in this book will stand the test of our times is the one question that matters. We will not know whether they will or not until we have tried them. If the life patterns described here work in producing the harmony, joy, peace, and self-giving love that make us willing to cooperate for the well-being of all, there must be *water* there! This to the scientifically minded person is all the evidence needed. It is hoped these pages may open up the plugged channels that lead to the rivers of the water of life for many of the current generation! *The crucial test is whether or not we find water! If we want the fruits, we also must want and develop the roots.*

Disciplines That Lead to New Perspectives

Christian prayer and worship, as practiced by Jesus throughout his life, point to the ways any of us may find the perspectives we need. Such prayer and worship, along with their accompanying disciplines of meditation, silence, contemplation, reading, and sharing with others, are the most costly action and priceless privilege known to humanity. They display the most creative, life-transforming perspective of which a human being is capable. Through them our spiritual roots may indeed reach the rivers of living waters and produce life with a new song in spite of the worst circumstances.

I said something like this in an address and was immediately dared by one of my hearers to prove my statement. Does the developing of spiritual roots of genuine faith in a regularly disciplined, intelligent approach to life *really* produce a life of love, peace, joy, and positive action in spite of the worst circumstances? I answered without hesitating, "Yes, I have found it so, and I can tell you of many others who know it is true."

"All right then," said my doubting friend, "how about a young person with cancer? I dare you to show how the spiritual disciplines of faith could do anything for such a person."

I responded with the story of a beautiful young woman of thirty-five, radiant, with an infectious gaiety and kindness that made her loved by many friends and adored by her husband. True, she was somewhat spoiled by the adulation, but in general she remained a naturally free and loving person. Although members of the church I served, she and her husband were generally too occupied with parties on Saturday night to get up for worship on Sunday. But one day, I was called to visit her in the hospital where she had undergone a hysterectomy.

When I entered the room, her face was the picture of despair. She had insisted her doctor, who was also our mutual friend, tell her the whole story. Yes, she had a malignancy. Yes, they would give her radium treatments, but the chances were ten to one against her recovery.

After she had told the story through many tears, she flared in anger, "Lance, I can't stand to think of what's ahead! Anything but cancer! What right does a good God have to permit such an affliction in me? I'm too young."

Bitter and humiliated, she resented God, life, and her husband. Then she calmed down and, with a piteous cry for help, said what any normal, secular-minded person would say in such a situation.

"Tell me how I can meet it, but don't ask me to pray about it. And don't tell me how its going to develop my character! I don't want to die. I want to live!"

I won't go through the long hours of conversation we shared together over the next few weeks. I told her about the nature of God as I believed is revealed in Jesus Christ and the framework of frailty with freedom in which we are to be reconciled to God.

Through her eagerness and openness she began to understand the meaning of prayer as Jesus prayed— prayer that is a response and a relationship rather than a magical attempt to master the powers of the universe for our own benefit. She learned prayer as the way to new perspective and illumination resulting in honest combat between God and her self-demands.

One day she submitted, not to me or to a vengeful God, but to the loving purpose of a Heavenly Creator whom she could not understand but whom she could trust. She did not have answers, but she had *the* answer—a confidence in the Eternal Love that held her in life and in death. When she said yes to the greatness and majesty of a love so great that even the cross could not defeat it, she won the victory over her own bitterness and resentment and then over her fears. She discovered that "perfect love banishes fear" (1 John 4:18, NEB).

I have never seen a more remarkable change take place in the mind and spirit of any person. She was as eager as a child packing for a long journey to a beautiful mountain resort. I could not tell her what was ahead because I had not been there and knew no one who had. I could not even give her definite proof that it was there. I did lead her through the thinking of great spirits such as St. Francis, John Wesley, the Apostle Paul, and the writer of the Book of Revelation.

Her little body wasted away until she was a bit of wrinkled skin and bones; yet from that body her spirit shown like an incandescent light. Her husband and her friends were the most astonished at the new Peggy. She talked with them freely and unaffectedly about her faith and the future. Her utter lack of fear and her patience under the indignities and pains of her illness made her seem like a bright ray of hope in a darkened world full of the heavy mists of hopelessness and despair. Hers was a perspective on life that opened the door for her friends who had valued pleasure and things above all else. Now some of them saw meanings and values that were to change their whole approach to life. A community of hopeful new believers resulted, and the circle of friends among whom she had moved lost much of its artificial gaiety and became a circle of love and joy.

At her memorial service there was a light shining through her life and witness that no darkness could put out. I can honestly say that I learned as much from her as I have from almost any other person I ever knew—in a short six months! But what of the length of life when seen through the perspective of faith? It is eternal!

Perspective Is the Way You Look at Things

As the familiar nursery rhyme describes it:

> Pussy cat, pussy cat, where have you been?
> I've been to London to see the Queen.
> Pussy cat, pussy cat, what saw you there?
> I saw a little mouse run under her chair.

Do you see life as the cat who went to London to see the queen but came back telling only of the mouse under her chair? Or do you see it as a human being who audaciously believes in some strange but real way that you are a child of the mighty God, Creator of all this multiverse with its billions of galaxies of suns and stars and, as many astronomers declare possible, hundreds or even thousands of planets where life is much further developed than on our earth?

True perspective is the capacity to see things in their *true relationships*, the ability *to discern* what is *primary* and what is *secondary*. On the other hand, perspective may be false, partial, twisted, and illusory. It may be as inadequate as the perspective of a flea in the wrinkle of an elephant's skin. Every time the elephant takes a mud bath, no doubt the flea thinks the world is coming to an end!

How desperately we need a true perspective from which to see ourselves and our world with our poor overburdened, anxious, striving, self-pitying, frustrated, and depressed lives! We need to see things as they are in the light of reality that God sees, not as our little ego-centered selves would see them! This requires the ability to see above ourselves, which is our holiest and most precious possibility as human beings.

We need what the old southern preacher had, who, in spite of the loss of his family in a fire and a multitude of troubles, was the most cheerful person in the community. When someone asked him how it happened, he said, "Well, I'll tell you. When I begin to feel sorry for myself, I just crawl up on a fence and watch myself pass by and I just die a'laughin'."[7]

Christian prayer and worship at their best are that fence on which even the most despairing of us may crawl and begin to see things we never saw before. It is here that we find the power to sing a new song, to laugh at our follies and fears, and to begin a new approach to life.

This ability to accept ourselves in a conscious, intelligent relationship to God, resulting in an increasingly true perspective, is the essence of genuine Christian prayer and worship as countless great spirits through the centuries testify. It is not some difficult game of manipulating God, of getting God to do what we want. It is not an escape, not wasted breath and time, but it is the power to see the truth about ourselves and our world, to accept it, and to act on it with joy and victory. As Dag Hammarskjöld expressed so clearly:

> How could this moral sense [upon which society depends] have escaped withering away, had it not constantly been watered by the feeder stream of power that issues from those who have forgotten themselves in God?[8]

These are not the words of a misty-eyed religious fanatic but of one of the most creative, well-integrated, and fearless statesmen of the twentieth century.

The Power of True Perspectives

The potent power of true perspective is the one thing so often missing in our lives and society and even in the life of the church. This is the reason for the crisis in so many of our homes and cities, in our nation and world, as well as in the church. For even in the church we have division, discouragement, crippling doubts, a strange cannibalism where Christians, members of a family, and citizens peck, peck, peck at each other with the absurd idea that the best way to save the nation or the church or the home is to destroy it. We have hostile gaps between citizens and government leaders; between clergy and laity, conservatives and liberals, advocates of social action and individual religion; between young and old, black and white, between those who empha-

size worship and those who push action. All such cannibalistic self-destruction would be impossible if we
really agonized over true issues and needs and understood the motives of people we condemn and seek to destroy by words if not by guns. This lack of true
perspective results in losing the very things we love
most. Here is the tragedy of a father and mother separated from and cursing the rebellious son or daughter
whom they feel has betrayed them. Here is the pastor or
lay member of the church rejecting and destroying the
church without understanding that it can be redeemed
and redemptive! How lacking in insight when we fail to
see with Paul that "if you bite and devour one another
take heed that you are not consumed by one another"
(Gal. 5:15, REV).

The strange paradox of the church, as well as of other
institutions of our society, is that never have so many
pastors and members, leaders and citizens worked
harder for their ideal with less results!

Something essential is missing. What is it? Some say,
"Work harder, get with it." Certainly those who say they
believe in the love of God and humanity need to realize
more clearly that to accept this love means sacrifice and
effort. But the real truth is that the word *sacrifice* is almost
gone from our vocabulary. We do not seem to be willing
to pay the price to bridge the gaps, to be reconcilers, to
act with love. Even when we do work, it is devoid of
power, meaning, and joy. Our work is often ineffective
because it is done out of a sense of duty rather than out
of overflowing love and confidence. We are lacking the
song of new perspective of the grace and truth in Christ.
As a result of our lack, the gaps are wider, our frustra-
tions and futility more pronounced, and our doubts and
cannibalistic infighting more destructive.

One of the widest gaps is between those who believe
that the changes so desperately needed to remove the
evils that curse humankind must come from without,
through changing the system and the institutions of society, and, on the other hand, those who believe that the
changes must come from within—the old battle between
social and personal salvation. An editor of *Psychology To-*

day in an interview with Arthur Koestler, former Communist turned author and playwright, asked which one of these approaches he favored. Koestler answered:

> Neither method has ever been successful. One way leads to the Inquisition and the purges, the other to passive submission to the bayonet, to feces in the gutter and to trachoma. . . . We keep trying various forms of compromise, but we've never been able to synthesize the saint and the revolutionary. . . . It's like asking a bird to become a fish![9]

I would like to ask Mr. Koestler if he has ever heard of Jesus or Paul, of St. Francis or Wesley, of Frank Laubach or Pope John XXIII? The synthesis between the saint and the revolutionary has taken place in many times and places in human history. For such persons humanity is greatly indebted and for many more such persons we are in desperate need. This synthesis is the result of the perspective of Christlike love that unites the inner and the outer. Prayer and worship combined with social action result in wise, constructive power rather than the opposite.

The crisis of today in church, in government, and in home is due to this lack of perspective in which the saint (God's dedicated person) and the revolutionary are made one. In the church, this lack shows most clearly in two contrasting styles or emphases. The first emphasis is on activism, in which the only important thing is acting for social justice. The other style of church life has a feeling that if such action is too costly and undesirable, one should forget it and do "church work" such as bazaars, committee meetings, and suppers.

The sad fact is that for many on both sides there is a complete or near complete cessation of prayer and worship. Some try feebly to continue the old pieties, but with great confusion as to their meaning and value. Prayer and worship are dubbed "unscientific," "other worldly," "irrelevant," "a waste of time and energy." Get with it and do something.

This approach is like the story of the people in a lifeboat that was pitching about in the high waves and almost going under. One young man cried, "Let us pray." The tough old bos'n called, "Let the little feller pray, but you man the oars!" So a great many would say that there is no need or value in prayer and worship—"just man the oars and get with it!"

Look where this has led us. So many have lost this greatest privilege and power—the understanding of who we are, the reality of the ruling love of God in Christ accepted and celebrated in life and action, the required balancing of interior and exterior, rational and irrational in human life.

This precious confidence in the deep reality of the love that makes all this possible enabled St. Francis to pray and live out his prayer with such profound influence on the Europe of his time and on our own time.

> Lord, make me an instrument of Thy peace.
> Where there is hate, may I bring love;
> Where offense, may I bring pardon;
> May I bring union in place of discord;
> Truth, replacing error;
> Faith, where once there was doubt;
> Hope, for despair;
> Light, where was darkness;
> Joy to replace sadness.
> Make me not to so crave to be loved as to love.
> Help me to learn that in giving I may receive;
> In forgetting self, I may find life eternal.

Why are so many of us who call ourselves Christians such poor peacemakers, such poor reconcilers—open scandals and not-so-funny jokes to the world that hears our fine words and noble professions? We can fool neither ourselves nor the world. We really haven't been with it! Why? Largely because of our failure to understand and meet the crisis in prayer and worship which is really a crisis in faith. Why pray when God is not real? Why worship a dim globular blur or an integrating principle? Having lost the reality of God, many of us have lost our own identity—our true perspective. We want the "fruit of the Spirit . . . love, joy, peace, patience, . . . self-control" (Gal. 5:22–23, RSV), but so often we do *not* want the roots from which grows the fruit of the Spirit, or at least we do not know how to grow these roots.

My experience, like that of so many others who have found Christian faith the source of all hopeful action, is that Christian prayer and worship are not primarily an enigma or a problem to be solved. Rather they are privileges to be accepted and lived.

Without such realistic prayer, someone who goes out to act, even at great cost to self and others, may indeed succeed only in killing the things that that person loves. Paul described accurately the futility of social action when it is self-righteous. "I may give away everything I have, and even give up my body to be burned—but if I have not love, this does me no good" (1 Cor. 13:3, TEV). Such action without the perspective of honest, open, obedient prayer, which makes wise, strong love possible, will do no one any good, except perhaps the ones who profit temporarily from the actions. But often even the disadvantaged and the poor for whom we seek justice find more harm than good in our self-sacrificing acts.

Without adequate perspective, though our objectives are good, our means will likely be less than adequate and even harmful to ourselves and to our cause.

True Perspective Includes Both Love and Justice

In the life of Christ and in the realism of human life, the two can never be separated. The teachings of Christ contain both; they are neither soft and sentimental nor harsh and dominating. Love without justice is naïve, and justice without love is destructive. A prophetic ministry by itself is always harmful unless it is joined with a pastoral concern in which love enables us to accept with mercy those who are unjust even while we seek to remove the injustice. The television special celebrating the one hundredth anniversary of Abraham Lincoln's death described Lincoln as "hard as a granite rock and soft as a drifting fog." Lincoln cared deeply for those whom the Civil War hurt even as he was in the middle of trying to bring it to an end and as he wrote the Emancipation Proclamation. Clearly, if there had been enough loving justice, there would have been no Civil War. How precious and how desperately needed is the perspective of Christlike love!

There is, therefore, no more destructive creature on earth than the self-righteous reformer who is narrow, vindictive, and unable to keep from killing the very thing that reformer loves. The only other creature who is equally destructive is the self-righteous pietist who escapes from social action into a dream world of familiar piety and turns the whole mess over to God! Both the self-righteous "saint" and the unloving revolutionary lose what they really seek to gain.

We have life only when we realize that Christian prayer and worship are our finest work and that our work, no matter how well intentioned, is empty and futile without worship at its best. The two belong together and cannot be separated if we are to be ready for the song of new perspectives that can lead to creative action. Arthur Koestler is right. The saint and the revolutionary must be synthesized; but his hope for combining the two by finding a pill we can swallow that will unite the inner and outer brain of a person, thus disciplining the brutish selfishness and passion that prevent loving cooperation, would be laughable if it were not so sad. Salvation by chemistry or electronics is a hopeless booby trap, a vain detour that fails because it depersonalizes both humanity and the Source of Life. Reality to which we give the name of God is not impersonal at the center. Neither are the billions of small yet living units which we call *"human beings"—man* and *woman.*

Perspectives on Personal Relationships

Seeing the love, the quality of joy, the creative peace, the victory over temptation and evil in Jesus' life, his disciples said, "Lord, teach us to pray" (Luke 11:1, NEB). In other words, they were saying, "Teach us your secret. Tell us how to pray as you do, so that we may live as you do." And Jesus answered in the words that begin the Lord's Prayer. "When you pray, say, 'Father, thy name be hallowed; thy kingdom come'"

(Luke 11:2, NEB). What did Jesus mean by these time-honored words? Countless books, sermons, and critical analyses have been written about them, and I shall not try to compete with these worthy undertakings. I do want us to look, however, at these familiar words to see what they say to us concerning the needed perspective for the personal relationships that include the highest, deepest reality we call God and the little realities of our human selves.

Coming to the truest perspective of reality is the first requirement for life in any age. God is the name we give to the nature of reality at its highest and deepest—the center of all being. But what is this?

Jesus called this center of reality *Father,* or *Abba,* the Aramaic word for daddy or papa or Ab, as the Hebrew child spoke it. What a breathtaking leap of faith! At once we recognize this word *Abba* as a symbol representing a mighty mystery. Perhaps you do not like the word *father* because your father was a bad one. Nevertheless the fact that you can think of what a good father ought to be points to the validity of *father* as a good symbol of highest reality. The nature of God—Reality in and through all—is indeed a mystery and can never be contained or described in any one word or set of words, much less in pictures. If we could put it into words or pictures, what we describe would not be God, but rather an idol, as indeed many of the words and representations of God have become.

One thing in the life and victorious death of Jesus and the continuing life of our risen Lord we, by faith, can see is God's intention! This is the heart and core of our Christian faith and commitment. God's nature and character and something of God's ongoing purpose are supremely revealed in the human Jesus, in his earthly life, in his resurrected life over the centuries, and through his followers. The New Testament understood Jesus' words, "Our Father," to mean "the Father of our Lord Jesus Christ." Here, we believe, is a true perspective on our own lives. As the Roman Catholic theologian Professor Edward Schillebeeckx puts it in the now classic book *Christ the Sacrament of the Encounter with God:*

His human love is the human embodiment of the redeeming love of God. . . . The man Jesus, as the personal visible realization of the divine grace of redemption, is *the* sacrament . . . because this man, the Son of God himself, is intended by the Father to be in his humanity the only way to the actuality of redemption. . . . Personally to be approached by the man Jesus was, for his contemporaries, an invitation to a personal encounter with the life-giving God, because personally that man was the Son of God. Human encounter with Jesus is therefore the sacrament of the encounter with God.[10]

When we pray *Our Father,* we mean at least that the ultimate mystery behind all things is concerned about us, is better, wiser, and stronger than the best human father or mother. Therefore, the truest relationship between us and God is *trust,* the kind of trust that Jesus had in the worst moments, even on the cross, as well as in those beautiful days on the mountainside. Our highest privilege and gift is to possess this trust and to see ourselves and the true value of our loved ones and even our enemies. Surely none of us who, from our hearts, says "Father" can conceive of God as one who would do less for us or treat us worse than we would our own children! This is clearly what Jesus meant when he said, "If you then, who are evil, know how to give good gifts to your children, how much more will your Father who is in heaven give good things to those who ask him!" (Matt. 7:11, RSV). "Or what man of you, if his son asks him for bread, will give him a stone? Or if he asks for a fish, will give him a serpent?" (Matt. 7:9–10, RSV).

"Nothing can be good in him which evil is in me," cried Whittier. And so by faith we pray with our Lord, "Our Father, who is in the heaven of reality, hallowed, reverenced, adored be your name, your character, your purpose."

The supreme question to which the answer of our Christian faith gives priceless perspective is this: does the impersonal and nonrational rule and thereby frustrate the personal and the rational in our human existence? The basic insight that the prayer of our Lord declares is good news indeed: We are members of the

human family and truly akin to the Spirit who so won-
drously rules this universe, the gracious but strong
Father of our Lord Jesus Christ. We are related personally in a personal universe. And we have a song to sing
that lifts us out of self-pity and futility to hope and joy
and love!

This is truly the crucial affirmation upon which any
significant life depends. But how can we be sure? In the
very same way we are sure of the love of our human
father, mother, or any other human being. This is, *by being with them*.

"Oh," you say, "that is too simple. We can see them,
but God is unseen and incomprehensible." True up to a
point. The Old Testament does speak of God who is hidden. "Clouds and thick darkness are round about him"
(Psalm 97:2, RSV). "How long, O Lord? Wilt thou hide
thyself for ever?" (Psalm 89:46, RSV). "Oh, that I knew
where I might find him, that I might come even to his
seat! . . . Behold, I go forward, but he is not there; and
backward, but I cannot perceive him; on the left hand I
seek him, but I cannot behold him; I turn to the right
hand, but I cannot see him" (Job 23:3, 8–9, RSV).

Indeed, when Alexander the Great conquered Jerusalem, the first thing he did was to enter the Temple to see
this Yahweh, the God of the stubborn people he had
vanquished; but to his amazement and disgust there
was nothing to be seen. Their Yahweh was invisible!
Rightly so, for the inspired people of the Old Testament
refused to have any image or picture of God and much
of the time they did not even use a word to describe him.
When Moses encountered God at the burning bush and
asked by what name he should be called in warning
Pharaoh, he was told, "I AM; that is who I am. Tell them
that I AM has sent you to them" (Exod. 3:14, NEB).

Encounter with God

"In the fullness of time," "the Word [that creates,
sustains, and cares for all things] became a human
being and full of grace and truth, lived among us. We
saw his glory. . . . No one has ever seen God. The only

Son, who is the same as God and is at the Father's side, he has made him known" (John 1:14, 18, TEV).

As the early disciples of Jesus looked back over his life and the meaning of his death and resurrection, they were sure of one thing: he was a man among humanity. In his humanity there was something priceless being said and done. It was left to the aging John, writing in the Gospel bearing his name, to summarize most clearly the significance of Jesus, whom they believed to be the Christ. John used the name *the Word* for creating, sustaining, caring God of all things as he described what had happened in Jesus as the Son of God and the Son of man.

Yes, God is hidden in fullness and glory, for no mere finite man could bear to see God in complete totality. Even the God in our Lord Jesus Christ is still infinite mystery, unfathomable in all the glory. He is "not to be encountered in the way in which we encounter other human beings."[11] But what these words about the encounter with the human Jesus, as the visible representation of the invisible, revealing the nature and purpose of God tell us is that the mystery of the hidden and unseen God is of the same kind as that of the mystery of human personality. For "are we so sure that we really do encounter the neighbor?"[12] What we see when we see our loved ones in visible form is not the deepest truth about them, but only the external. We do not see the essence, but only the manifestation of the loved one's nature—the loved one's character, attitude, and acts. As Joseph Pieper says it, in *The Silence of St. Thomas,* "The creature as creature is mystery to us, and somewhere, I think, St. Augustine has said that it is only in eternity that we will really see the neighbor, when we see him in God."[13] But we experience our neighbors as we are with them and witness their acts, hear their words, feel their touch. We come to know the real persons through what they do and say. "It is in his body and through his body that a man is open to the outside and that he makes himself present to his fellow man."[14] So it is that, supremely in Jesus, God is present with us.

Through the centuries there have been human per-

sonalities that were translucent with the light of some reality greater than themselves. The love of St. Francis
made the love of Christ a reality for countless thousands
because he so completely identified himself with the
love of the human Jesus. If you have ever had anyone
near you who loved with even a small part of such love,
you would know as I do that the human word spoken by
that person is indeed the word of the eternal love. Whatever the meaning of the stigmata—the signs of the nail
prints tradition describes as on the feet and hands of
Francis—his life truly bore the marks of Jesus. In him
Jesus lived all over again and through him lived the eternal love of God! So, to some degree, with all persons
who submit themselves willingly and obediently to the
spirit of the Christ.

I think of my mother, who continued to identify her
life with Christ from the earliest time I knew her until
her death at the age of seventy-six. As I think of my own
belief in the love of God, I am sure it was mediated to me
first of all through her. When I was a baby, she held me
in her arms and prayed that God's love would be seen in
my life, whether as a minister of Christ's gospel or in
whatever vocation I chose. But she never told me this
until, at the age of eighteen, I wrote her of my decision to
live by faith in Christ and to study for the Christian ministry.

She never failed to write or to share with me something of her vision of the needs of the world and of what
Christ could mean if only people understood. She made
no parade of her faith, but many times I came upon her
praying and saw a light on her face, sometimes tears in
her eyes, and I knew hers was a real encounter with a
reality greater than she could describe or I could ever
understand.

So the mystery of who God is and what love is may be
known with assurance in our experience of God—God's
manifestation in Jesus Christ and in those who have
caught his spirit. So *Christian prayer and worship are being
with God as revealed in Jesus Christ, in acts of intelligent faith*.
There may or may not be the desired feeling, though
feelings generally follow. Ecstasy and visions are not the

proof, for prayer and worship are acts of faith as we are with God in the encounter with Christ whose spirit is mediated to us through the human Jesus and through others who have lived in his spirit. We call this encounter prayer on the individual side and worship on the corporate side as we join with others in seeing with our spiritual sight and celebrating and acting on what we see.

The True Perspective on Who We Are

The perspective on who God is, revealed in the Son, gives us the priceless perspective on who we are. When you pray, say, "*Our* Father." What a world of difference when we say *our*. There is no life of freedom and joy in isolation, but only in loving mutuality. The sweet mystery of life is wise, strong, giving love. "For the whole law is fulfilled in one word, 'You shall love your neighbor as yourself'" (Gal. 5:14, RSV). "Love those who hate you, love even as I have loved you"—thus we may summarize Jesus' perspective on our fellow human beings derived from his faith in God!

True mutuality of love is possible only as our own masks are torn off and as the walls of distrust, suspicion, and hostility are torn down between us. And this is possible only as I love and trust you as I know you love and trust God. The fact is that we cannot love others and ourselves rightly unless we are loved by One who is greater and higher than we. To be able to see into other persons' needs and hurts, to be merciful, kind, and constructive when we dislike and even hate their evil actions, and then to love them is the first necessity for life and peace in the home, in the church, between races, and in the world. It comes only as we accept ourselves as loved and forgiven by God. In the security of this love, then we may love. The word *love,* as used here, does not mean sentimental affection but mutual respect, strong, wise, constructive, self-giving good will, even when the persons loved are unlovable, even hateful! Possessive, desiring love alone destroys; wise, strong, giving love creates and heals.[15]

Alan Paton, in his book *Instrument of Thy Peace,* uses the prayer of St. Francis to make one of the clearest statements I have read on the necessity for the right kind of prayer as the channel to becoming an instrument of peace in the world. In his prologue, he says he is writing

> for those who do not wish to be cold in love, and who know that being cold in love is perhaps the worst sin of them all; for those who wish to keep their faith bright and burning in a dark and faithless world.[16]

He admits that he is in

> unrepayable debt to Francis of Assisi, for when I pray his prayer, or even remember it, my melancholy is dispelled, my self-pity comes to an end, my faith is restored, because of this majestic conception of what the work of a disciple should be.
>
> So majestic is this conception that one dare no longer be sorry for oneself. This world ceases to be one's enemy and becomes the place where one lives and works and serves.[17]

Why this creative response? Because we accept ourselves as loved by the steadfast love of Christ, and therefore we are not primarily concerned about getting other people to love us. Surely that is the heart and secret of true perspective so desperately needed in our human lives today.

Our Ladder of Sins

Our trouble is that we all have a *ladder of sins,* or whatever *name* you want to call our deceitful, selfish, proud, and hurtful attitudes and acts. We may not be on the top rung of this ladder with the great saints, but neither are we on the bottom rung! We look down on those beneath us for, after all, there is always somebody much worse, we think, and to gossip about them somehow makes us feel better. Self-righteous morality (looking down on others) is as harmful, and sometimes more so, as the more obvious sins.

Jesus said to the most religious people of his day, the Pharisees, whose morals were impeccable, according to their interpretation of the law, "Truly, I say to you, the tax collectors and the harlots go into the kingdom of God before you" (Matt. 21:31, RSV). No wonder they were angry, for they, like us, did not like to have their ladders of superiority torn down. They were unable to laugh at themselves and their pretensions.

We need a true perspective to see ourselves as we are in God's sight. Our perspectives are always so partial; we have only a knothole view of life! So often, like Snoopy, who lies on top of his doghouse viewing the whole world in superior disdain, we do not recognize the difficult truth about our own lives. From a true perspective, we are able to be honest before God, ourselves, and others.

Perspectives That Bring Life or Death

Only when I see myself in the mirror of Christ's loving goodness do I see the infinite possibilities of my life, only about one-twentieth of which, at best, will be realized unless I have an adequate discipline of prayer and meditation and worship with full openness to truth. Then and then only am I able to pray with honesty and wholehearted commitment, "Thy kingdom come, thy will be done in my life as in the realms of heavenly reality."

The fact we need now to recognize is that God's kingdom has come and will continue to come in the future. God's rule is here, though it is not acknowledged and understood by most people. We come to see that the only way things will work is according to God's will and way. This is the meaning of the old familiar words, "Our Father who art in heaven." Heaven is not only on some far-off star in the billionth galaxy. Heaven is wherever God is accepted and God's rule obeyed. Hell is wherever God's presence is unrecognized. When I am unwilling to say yes to God's purposes and seek to rule myself, I am in hell—the insanity of self-centeredness. It is easy to see this in others, but difficult in ourselves. Only as we learn to pray and worship honestly in God's

presence and only as we are willing to burn up our fa-
vorite ladder of sins from which we look down on others
can we be whole and free, able to help rather than destroy the things and persons we love most!

To pray "Thy kingdom come" requires surrender of
my kingdom. The fact that I have not done this is my
problem. This is the reason for the hurt feelings, the in-
jured pride, and the pain so many "good Christians"
have. Here is the reason the best-intentioned crusader,
reformer, and revolutionary so often fails. "*My* Kingdom come. *My* will be done" is the prayer we really are
praying, irrespective of the words we use.

Arthur B. Rhinow gives an imagined conversation between the Lord and Cain which points to our tragic situation.

> LORD—An offering from you, Cain? What do you
>   bring?
> CAIN—Of the fruits of the field.
> LORD—I gave you that. Have you nothing that is really
>   yours?
> CAIN—My arms, my limbs.
> LORD—All that was given you and will be taken from
>   you, Cain.
> CAIN—What then is truly mine?
> LORD—What you can keep forever.
> CAIN—That would be nothing but myself.
> LORD—Give me yourself.
> CAIN—Alas, I love myself.

But this answer is only a dodge to hide the real truth.
Cain did not, and neither do we without a new perspective, love the true self. It is this imagined picture of self
that we love. We cannot truly love ourselves until we see
that we are loved by God. Only when we love ourselves
as God loves us can we quit fighting our true selves and
pray that the kingdom will come in truth, in love, in
peace—in me as in the heaven of reality!

One morning a thrush flew through the open door of
my Vermont study and was frightened by my presence.

Seeing the large picture window, she flew against the glass trying to escape. Time and time again she hurled herself against the glass only to fall back bruised and broken. I was unable to help her until finally she was so weak and hurt she let me guide her to freedom. As I watched her fly away I wondered, "Will not God do as much for me?" I recalled Jesus' words, "Fear not, . . . you are of more value than many sparrows" (Matt. 10:31, RSV). "And not one of them will fall to the ground without your Father's will" (Matt. 10:29, RSV).

I realized that this is a parable of every one of us, and of humankind. We are beating our life wings against the false glass of our own built-in picture of life that beckons with alluring promises of freedom from boredom, littleness, and rejection. The result of our struggles is only to fall back time and again, bruised and broken by the lovelessness, inferiority, hostility, and fear that come from our inability to see the truth about our lives and world. We are looking at life through the wrong perspective. No wonder people are rebelling at the rigidities of the perspective of materialistic science and high technology just as they reject the rigid theological claims of proud self-righteousness. Someday we will learn, perhaps through much suffering, that there is no way out through our own self-made windows.

It will be a happy day indeed when we stop fighting God and our true selves! We will become humble and secure when we are willing to be truly human. The Lord of truth and love will pick us up and turn us loose into the blue sky of freedom to be our true selves. We will lose our self-pity and hostility and begin to share with God in making our homes, our churches, our communities, and our world places where the eternal, loving reality is acknowledged and accepted.

Such is the priceless meaning and privilege of prayer and worship as perspective. From them come illumination, acceptance, caring involvement, and sacrifice with celebration!

Our Father who art in heaven—the heaven of highest reality,

Thy Kingdom come—not mine.
Thy will be done—not mine, in my home and in my
    world,
As it is in all your great and glorious universe.

4

The Costly Disciplines
of Illumination

Honesty Before God the Reality

O happy day! It is a happy day when we stop fighting the God of reality, the reality of our true selves, and the reality of the universe as it is rather than as we wish it were! For then, though it may have to be done in darkness and without visible sight or proof, we begin to say yes and amen to life. We demonstrate *"a willingness to let things be as they are* [at least as the given, the starting point]."[1] Meister Eckhart describes this kind of prayer as *"letting go and letting be."*

> The ultimate experience of letting go is an experience of letting be. Letting God be God. . . . Letting oneself be oneself and letting others be themselves. Letting things be things and letting God be God and in things. . . . It is a state of being open and sensitive. It means, says Eckhart, to be "receptive of all spirit."[2]

Then we are praying with Jesus: "The Son of God, Christ Jesus, proclaimed among you . . . was never a blend of Yes and No. With him it was, and is, Yes. He is the Yes pronounced upon God's promises, every one of them. That is why, when we give glory to God, it is through Christ Jesus that we say 'Amen'" (2 Cor. 1:19–20, NEB).

Saying yes through Jesus Christ enables us to accept ourselves as of "more value than many sparrows" (Matt. 10:31, RSV), as accepted and loved by God—

amazing thought! We can stop trying to fly like a de-
luded bird through the window glass of our own
self-centered values and demands. We are open to the
truth, humble and secure; and, therefore, we are free to
be our true selves. This miraculous transformation from
slavery to freedom has happened to thousands in every
age. It is taking place now in hundreds of youth who
have been on heroin and other drugs. It is happening to
countless adults who have been addicted to alcohol, race
prejudice, and material things, who have grown old and
weary fighting themselves.

How does this infinitely desirable state come to be in
which obviously life is at its best? To summarize what
has been said before and to indicate another step: Christian prayer and worship at their best are the most creative and productive actions known to humanity. They
are the roots of the tree of life that reach down to the rivers of living water. This living water is the grace of God,
who gives us our most precious gifts, especially the gift
of a true perspective, the ability to see our lives and our
world and others about us as they really are, as God sees
them and not as we might picture them. This kind of
prayer and worship makes us open to receive the gift.

In the last chapter, we considered the insights given in
the first part of the Lord's Prayer. For some professing
Christians, the words are worn slick with familiarity.
They are thought of by secularists as old and dusty
words from another world so unlike ours as to be of no
value. *Abba-Father,* however, will never be an old dusty
word so long as there are loving parents and surrogate
parents willing to sacrifice themselves in strong, wise
love for their children. Indeed, I must reaffirm my
choice of the highest symbols or images we can think of
to represent the highest and deepest reality. Unques-
tionably, for me, the personal is infinitely above the impersonal, for the personal, the experience each of us is
given, is the call to master and control the impersonal.
So the word *Father* is a much more acceptable symbol
than unconscious force or integrating principle. The biblical writers make this clear. "The government will be
upon his shoulder, and his name will be called 'Won-

derful Counselor, Mighty God, Everlasting Father, Prince of Peace'" (Isa. 9:6, RSV). "'And his name shall be called Emmanuel' (which means, God with us)" (Matt. 1:23, RSV).

These names assume infinitely more value in our scientific age of technology than in the relatively simple ages preceding. For the impersonal is crowding out the personal, and this is one of the main reasons for so much meaninglessness in secular life. Can you imagine anyone in the depths of frustration and despair crying out for help to such impersonal forces: "Oh, Integrating Principles, give me wisdom!" "Oh, Cosmic Powers, give me your strength!" It is the crass uncaringness of an impersonal universe that presents us with our central predicament! If the cosmic powers are to support and strengthen us, they must be considered at least as personal as we are, that is, able to think and to care! Of course, these are symbols. *Anthropomorphic* is the word for thinking like a human. But how else can we think except in the highest symbols that have meaning to our human minds?

Therefore, these words—*Father, Counselor, Immanuel* (God with us)—and the deep reality they represent are truly the best hope for the people who sit in a greater darkness and the shadow of a more horrible death than could have been imagined in the time of Isaiah.

High technology and the fallout of addiction to things, money, sex, alcohol, or drugs leave us more vulnerable to despair than humankind has ever been before. We have an aloneness in the vastness of our multiverse that cannot be met by scientific or mathematical theorems or engineering devices.

Here, then, with reverence and awe, the summation of humanity's highest way of addressing and committing itself to God the reality:

Abba-Father who is in the heaven of reality, hallowed, revered be your name of love, your signature of compassion as written in the very constitution of the universe and supremely in the life and death of your Son on the cross of infinite love, but also written large in all

human life—your will, not mine, be done. Your kingdom, not mine, come!

Illumination

Such an intelligent perspective on the highest reality
opens up another of the springs of life which I am calling *illumination*—light in our darkness. Costly light it is
indeed, not only to God who gives it, but to us who
receive it, but most priceless and necessary for
constructive and loving life in any age!

How difficult it is to be honest with ourselves, not
only when we are young but even more so as we get
older. How very little we know of ourselves! How small
indeed was Simon Peter's knowledge of himself! In the
last hours with his teacher and friend before Jesus' betrayal and crucifixion, Peter had bragged, "Lord, why
cannot I follow you now? I will lay down my life for you"
(John 13:37, RSV). The record does not describe the
scene, but I am sure Jesus looked deep into Peter's eyes
as he answered with compassionate but realistic understanding, "Will you lay down your life for me? Truly,
truly, I say to you, the cock will not crow, till you have
denied me three times" (John 13:38, RSV).

Can you imagine what went on in Simon Peter's mind
both then and later as "the Lord turned and looked
at Peter"? Peter was standing in the outer court of
Caiaphas's palace, having denied his Lord just as Jesus
had said he would! What agony of mind Peter must have
had as his friend and master was dying on the cross and
then was laid in the tomb! Tradition has it that his hair
turned gray during these terrible hours. He realized not
only the sufferings of Jesus, but for the first time he
looked into the depths of himself and saw what he truly
was—a miserable traitor to all that he really wanted to be
and thought he was. He had not only denied his Lord,
but he had denied what he knew was his true self!

The story does not end here, for him or for us. If it did,
we would be creatures of unmitigated despair, for we
have all denied and betrayed our Lord and our true
selves, over and over again. The story goes on to the

scene by the lake that morning when Peter met the risen Lord. I think Jesus put his hands on Peter's shoulders and looked into his eyes as he said, "Simon, son of John, do you love me more than these?" (John 21:15, RSV). I think he meant, "more than these inner demands that you be a 'big shot,' successful, recognized, and important—do you really love me more than these? If you do, then feed my sheep."

From that hour, Peter ceased his bragging, self-centered ways and became more and more the "Rock" that his new name implied. He was selected by the other disciples as their leader. Though the old "Simon" in his nature made appearances several times through the years, Peter was faithful in feeding the sheep entrusted him by the Good Shepherd. Tradition tells of his martyrdom during the persecution of the Christians under Nero. As the soldiers proceeded to crucify him, the story goes, he asked that he be crucified with his head downward, "for I am unworthy to die as my Lord died."

Only when Simon, son of John, had become honest before God could he really become Peter the Rock, the son of God as Jesus saw him early in his discipleship! Only then could he truly pray with his Lord, "Our Father, thy kingdom come, thy will be done in me and through me, no matter the cost!" Only then could he become the mighty leader of the fearless, scattered band of disciples that began a new era of creative hope in the life of humankind.

Christian prayer and worship, meditation and thinking, at their best are accepting a truer perspective on our lives in the presence of eternal Love ruling all. Such times are moments of illumination, when at last we get honest before God and see ourselves and our world more nearly in the light of reality.

Obviously most of us are like Simon Peter. Before we are ready for the costly prayer that brings illumination, we must go through suffering; but the suffering must be seen in the light of the love that did not stop even at the cross. For then and only then can we be willing to accept the pruning knife of the Divine Gardener. Jesus indicated this need in the parable of the vine and the branches which he taught his disciples in their last night together. "I am the real vine, and my Father is the gardener. Every barren branch of mine he cuts away; and every fruiting branch he cleans, to make it more fruitful still. . . . The withered branches are heaped together, thrown on the fire, and burnt" (John 15:1–2, 6, NEB). As Phillips translates part of this unusual parable, "Now, you have already been pruned by my words. You must go on growing in me [subjecting your lives to more pruning] and I will grow in you" (John 15:3–4).

Costly Pruning

Pruning time is a costly time. Anyone who· has ever grown roses or grapes knows that when the leaves are permitted to luxuriate and continue growing without pruning, there will be few or no roses or grapes. The excess foliage must be pruned away. Humanly speaking, we do not like pruning. It hurts. This is the main reason there is so little truly honest prayer before the Christ presence: we are afraid we will be hurt.

"Lord, a little pruning may be necessary, but surely not these beautiful branches! I am so proud of them. Surely not this! or this! or this!"

But God is the Divine Gardener, neither dead nor on a vacation. God loves us so much that we will not be allowed to settle for anything less than our fullest development. We are to bear the most abundant crop of love, joy, and creative peace, with patience and fortitude and concern, of which we are capable! For God knows that nothing else can really satisfy God's own creative purpose for us, or satisfy us and the fellow members of the heavenly family.

The difference between us as persons and the rose bushes and the grapevines is that roses and vines do not have any choice as to whether or not they are to be pruned. As children of the Father-Mother-Creator, we have two choices: either to go voluntarily to the Divine Gardener's pruning so that we may be more fruitful, or to delay the pruning, put it off, seek to escape for awhile. But if we choose this last way, the forced pruning will come eventually in the form of the loving judgment of the Divine Gardener, who will not let us go fruitless. Surely the God-Reality cares as much for us as gardeners do their vines!

This is indeed an appropriate parable of what is happening today. During the past seventy-five years, we've seen in our world the forced pruning of two world wars, the Korean War, the Cuban revolution, the war in Vietnam, the terrorism and slaughter of the innocent as well as the guilty in the Middle East and Central and South America and, even in our own country, the Great Depression of the 1930s and the continuing economic upheaval and suffering of unemployment. We have seen it in our broken homes, in crushed and wrecked lives, in once-idealistic youth and older persons destroying themselves in escape through drugs, suicide, or nihilism. We see it in the church that often forgets its reason for being and even in our own lives that are often so miserable and destructive rather than joyous and creative. This is the forced pruning—the loving judgment of a righteous Gardener!

Christian prayer, worship, and the other disciplines of the devoted spirit, rather than being an escape, are ways of voluntarily asking for the Gardener's shears to prune away the unnecessary foliage and dead vines in order that we may produce more fruit of love and peace and joy! With these kinds of disciplines accepted gladly, the forced pruning is unnecessary. Wise indeed is the person who can say with the poet Howard McKinley Corning,

> In February, when the sap's below
> The inattentive earth, I take my shears
> And prune away the too-audacious years.
> It's grapes I want, not mere leafy show.
> I trim the trailing year's growth to a span.
> . . . .
>
> It takes some fortitude to cut a vine
> . . . .
>
> Cutting the heart a little . . . as I cut mine.
> But since it's grapes I want, I understand
> How to rebuke the heart to fill the hand.[3]

How does one "rebuke the heart to fill the hand"? The trouble is we do not know our hearts. We recall again Jeremiah's words, "The heart is the most deceitful of all things, desperately sick; who can fathom it?" (Jer. 17:9, NEB). None of us likes to believe that. Indeed, we have plenty of cheerful humanists to tell us that people are innately good. All they need is better teaching, more information about themselves and those around them. But depth psychology, as I have previously pointed out, shows us the extent of our rationalizations and self-justifications, how we hide even from ourselves the real reasons for our negative, hurtful attitudes and acts. How easy to make ourselves believe that anything we want is good because we want it. As Jesus put it, "Wisdom is justified by all her children" (Luke 7:35, RSV).

How do we really get honest with ourselves before God who is the truth, the reality of life and of all things in this mysterious universe, who makes possible the glorious but costly illumination we need?

We gain the honesty by doing what Simon Peter did—putting Jesus Christ as Lord in the center of our attention. This is the reason Christians have always prayed, "through Jesus Christ, our Lord," "in the name of Jesus." For this is what Christian prayer and worship really are—getting a good look at ourselves and our world in the light of a clear day. In honest prayer we subject our innermost thoughts, desires, attitudes, and acts, as well as the attitudes and acts of others, to the light of Christ—the light that shines inexorably into the darkest and murkiest corners.

What a tremendous difference in Simon Peter before and after the crucifixion! Before, the center of his attention was himself—his needs, his "must-haves," the demands of the little lord Simon, whose deepest desires, conscious and unconscious, were to prove himself a big success in his own eyes and in the eyes of others, even to the little maid in the court of Caiaphas's palace! After the crucifixion and the terrible experience of seeing Jesus during his trial turn and look at him, the center of Peter's attention was on Christ. In the light of Christ's look,

Peter saw his little, unworthy, petty self as it really was. He hated what he saw enough to surrender it. Captured by the love of Christ he was able to become a new person—the "Rock" that Jesus had seen him as being.

Christian prayer and devotion—worship, contemplation, meditation—are meeting God in conscious, glad attentiveness in Christ.

First, we meet God in the story of the man Jesus, who lived, loved, suffered, was crucified, died, was buried, and rose again, becoming, through the will of the Divine Reality, the "universal power as the Master of history, the Lord of the universe."[4] It is this concentrated attention by Christians of every age on the saving event centering around the human Jesus that has produced such results in the use of the *Spiritual Exercises* of St. Ignatius of Loyola and the other creative disciplines of prayerful reading.

> The gospels do not simply give cold facts about our Lord; they record his words and actions as understood, selected, interpreted and *lived* by these privileged witnesses to the faith of the apostolic Church. . . . Because the sacred text conveys this revelation about Jesus of Nazareth incarnated in the reaction of faith of its sacred author (and of the Christian community that stands behind him), it is capable of producing a similar reaction of faith in the twentieth-century believer. . . . The final step . . . is the religious experience, the "saving event." . . . *The mystery must happen for me, to me.*[5]

The illumination of God's love in Christ has brought the meaning and value of human life to light, and in that light we see ourselves not only as we are, but as we can be. All over the world today men and women are finding themselves—their true selves—in their personal and group encounter with Jesus Christ. They no longer need to depend on dope or alcohol or recognition or material success for life! "The mystery has happened for me and to me!"

This mystery—the new illumination resulting in the new creation—happens to us not only by concentrating our attention on the simple, loving human Jesus; but from the time of Pentecost, we, like the early Christians, find the events in the life, death, and victory of Jesus our friend revealing the infinite love and victory of the eternal spirit whom Jesus taught us to call "Father." The New Testament Christians used interchangeably the words *Christ, Spirit of Jesus Christ,* and *Holy Spirit* to indicate that the great Creator had been made known in the life and spirit of their friend Jesus, and that now in his risen life, this eternal Christ was near to them in the Holy Spirit. Their Christ and ours is the Lord of history, who "directed the destinies of his church as well as of the entire universe."[6] The central conviction that moved the apostolic church, as it has vital Christians ever since, was "that Jesus Christ through his exaltation . . . has *not* been removed to some mythical existence beyond the furthest galaxy, but is *actually more dynamically present* in the world than ever he was when he walked the hills of Galilee."[7] He is not withdrawn but more actively and really present in the life and history of humanity than ever!

Christian prayer, therefore, is meeting the mighty God-Reality as made known in the historical man Jesus, who as the risen Christ is really present with us. Christ lives continually in our own spirits when we are open to him and in the spirits of the great and loving persons of all times and places.

How to Open Our Spirits

There are two ways in which we open our spirits to God. First, by thinking, consciously meditating on God's gracious goodness, majestic greatness, wisdom, and love, the continuing good news that lives in those who have the same Spirit. The first part of all genuine Christian prayer and worship is conscious attention on the nature of God. The opening address of the Lord's Prayer indicates this. "Our Father who art in heaven, hallowed be thy name."

> There's a wideness in God's mercy,
> Like the wideness of the sea;
> There's a kindness in his justice,
> Which is more than liberty.

. . . .

> For the love of God is broader
> Than the measure of man's mind;
> And the heart of the Eternal
> Is most wonderfully kind.[8]

Second, we meet him consciously by faith.

> Speak to Him, thou, for He hears, and Spirit
>   with Spirit can meet—
> Closer is He than breathing, and nearer than
>   hands and feet.[9]

Yes, but meeting God is no accident; we must consciously *will* to meet God. When our attention is joined with God's, we have the precious illumination we need. We begin to see ourselves and to enter into the new creation.

The hub of our problem is that we are never told how to acquire the truth of the illumined spirit. Some illumination may come from hypnotism and psychiatry, but even then there is some deeper mystery, some more adequate source. Is it by taking a trip on "angel dust" or other drugs? Is it by the way of contemplation made popular by Zen Buddhism? This is not the place to discuss the values and/or dangers of the mind-blasting produced by drugs, but I am convinced that the ecstasy for which our human spirits were made is not produced by cheap artificial methods. It will come only as our whole beings enter into a union with the sacrificial love that is at the center of all things. There will then be no hangover or withdrawal pains.

Certainly psychology, psychiatry, and the Eastern religions have much to teach us Christians about the use of our conscious attention. Douglas Steere tells the story of the Indian student who, after three years of study with an aged Hindu sage, came one morning as he was ready to return home. He asked his wise teacher, "Basalmi, I must now return home. Will you sum up for me your teachings on the way to enlightenment?" The old man took a piece of bamboo and wrote one word on the white inside of the bark, *attention*. The young man was disappointed. "Surely," he cried, "you have something

more to say to me than that!" The old man took the bark
again and wrote another time the same word, *attention*.
This time the student was almost angry, "Surely after
three years with you, there is more you have to say to me
of final wisdom than these two words!" Again the wise
old sage took the bamboo and wrote for the third time,
attention!

He was summing up the costly experience of the centuries: *The power to put our attention where we choose is the
greatest single fact of our human freedom!* In this we are different from rose bushes, grapes, and, so far as we know,
all other creatures on this planet. "This is our last great
freedom," says Viktor Frankl, Austrian psychiatrist, in
the story of his experience in the Nazi concentration
camp during World War II.[10] No matter what happens,
however evil or good, terrible or pleasurable the situation is, we still have the freedom to say, "I will" or "I
won't." *We are free to put our attention where we choose.*

This is the freedom that Paul says peculiarly belongs
to you who "delight yourselves in the Lord . . . and
never forget the nearness of your Lord" (Phil. 4:4, PHIL-
LIPS). "All that is true, all that is noble, all that is just and
pure, all that is lovable and gracious, whatever is excellent and admirable—fill all your thoughts with these
things . . . and the God of peace will be with you" (Phil.
4:8–9, NEB).

D. H. Lawrence writes:

> Thought [attention] is the welling up of unknown life
>   into consciousness.
>   .   .   .   .
> Thought is a man in his wholeness wholly attending[11]

Wholly attending to what? That is the question upon
which life, peace, and victory of the spirit depend—or
their opposites: our frustration, failure, inadequacy,
desperation. *Christian prayer is attending to Christ, putting
attention on him, not on our little selves with our problems,
our hurts and failures.* "All that came to be was alive with
his life, and that life was the light of men. The light

shines on in the dark, and the darkness has never mastered it" (John 1:4–5, NEB). "So the Word became flesh and dwelt among us—this Word that was in the beginning with God, the Word that is God, and is made flesh—we see his glory full of Grace and truth" (John 1:1–14, AUTHOR PARAPHRASE).

What kind of attention? Not pleading and begging, but looking with love and adoration, with reverence and awe and with something more—loving reflection and utter openness to see who we are, who our neighbor is, and who God is.

As Evelyn Underhill says so well, "What, in practice, the word Adoration implies [is] . . . awe-struck delight in the splendour and beauty of God. . . . This is adoration: not a difficult religious exercise, but an attitude of the soul."[12]

"But I don't feel like adoring! I certainly don't feel illumined. I see no light, only darkness. Nothing good and worthwhile seems possible to me. I am hostile, afraid, bitter, anxious, frustrated—I feel rotten, sick."

Yes, so do we all at times. That is our common human situation.

"But what do you do then?"

The answer of countless great spirits who have won the victory of faith in every age is: begin where you are. Begin with your discouragement, fear, bitterness, whatever. It isn't where your prayer, meditation, and worship *begin* but where they *end* that is important! Begin right where you are now.

How Do We Get Really Honest in Prayer and Worship?

Let me suggest three approaches from my own experience and from the accumulated experience of countless thousands over the ages.

The first requirement is to be still and *recognize that I am known by God*. There is One in this universe who knows me perfectly, all there is to know about me, *and still values and accepts me*. Now that is a priceless, won-

drous discovery, if I am open to it! The illumined words
of Psalm 139 (CHAMBERLAIN) say it in classic beauty and
simplicity.

> Lord, you have searched and known me;
> > You know my deeds and my thoughts,
> > > Discerning my purpose far in
> > > advance.
>
> . . . .
>
> How can I comprehend such wonders,
> > So far beyond my grasp!

Then the writer gets really honest.

> If only you would slay the wicked!
>
> . . . .
>
> Lord, I hate those who hate you—
>
> . . . .
>
> My hatred for them is complete.

Now we are getting his true thinking—the way he really
feels. But he does not stop there. He goes on with one of
the great prayers of all times. "Search me, O God, and
know my heart: try me, and know my thoughts: And
see if there be any wicked way in me, and lead me in the
way everlasting" (Ps. 139:23–24, KJV).

This is the kind of honesty that brings true illumination: to know that I am known by God! God knows me
and understands me, even if I don't. If the ancient
psalmist could open up mind and heart, how much
more can I open the deepest recesses of my being to
God's light. I who have seen revealed the wise loving
Father of our Lord Jesus Christ can pray:

> Show me my shell of false values and demands, the
> deeper hidden compulsions that hide the real me. Re-
> veal to me my heart—your picture of me—not only the
> false demands to which I have clung, but the true self
> waiting to be born.

This prayer in contemporary language is similar to the
ancient collect for purity.

Almighty God, unto whom all hearts are open, all desires known, and from whom no secrets are hid: cleanse the thoughts of our hearts by the inspiration of thy Holy Spirit, that we may perfectly love thee, and worthily magnify thy holy Name; through Christ our Lord. *Amen.*

This has always been our need, to stand in the clear day of Christ's light. Then we will begin to see *backward* into the stinking self-centeredness that causes our symptoms of pride, jealousy, greed, lust, fear, and hatred. But we will also look *forward* into the new being that is awaiting us with untold possibilities of giving-love, creative peace, "fortitude and patience with joy." The clear day comes when we learn what Jesus meant when he said, "If any man would come after me, let him deny himself ["leave self behind" (NEB)] and take up his cross and follow me" (Mark 8:34, RSV). The clear day came for Saul, the narrow, rigid, bigoted Pharisee, when he met Christ and began to be made over into Paul the apostle of love. "I die every day!" he wrote (1 Cor. 15:31, RSV). "I have been crucified with Christ; it is no longer I who live, but Christ who lives in me" (Gal. 2:20, RSV). The "old man," as Paul, Luther, and Wesley called this false self, has to die—once, twice, yes, daily so that the new creation in Christ may live!

How does this take place? Not by psychology or bootstrapping or do-it-yourself face-lifting, but by opening the self to the light. "You will know the truth, and the truth will make you free," said Jesus (John 8:32, RSV). How often this statement is misquoted. It follows Jesus' declaration of the condition for knowing the deepest and highest truth of all creation. "If you dwell within the revelation I have brought, you are indeed my disciples; you shall know the truth, and the truth will set you free" (John 8:31–32, NEB). Knowing the truth is possible only by adding another clause between the two in this well-known promise of Jesus—a clause necessary if we are to take into account the emphasis of his whole life and teachings. To paraphrase: You shall know the truth and the truth will first make you sick, but when you know that you are sick and need a physician, you may meet the Good Physician, and the truth he reveals shall set you free. If the Son sets you free, you shall be free indeed (cf. John 8:31–36; Luke 5:31–32).

From Jesus' own experience we get an illustration of what he meant by knowing the truth. Obviously Jesus did not have the "big-shot complex" that was Simon Peter's false picture of himself. But because of Jesus' very humanity, it was necessary for him to spend forty days in the wilderness wrestling with himself and the devil over the difference between the current expectations of his people and what God's expectations were. He also was struggling with the cost if he accepted that divine will. After the ecstatic experience at his baptism, when he saw further into the nature of reality than any other man has ever seen, he was given assurance by God. "This is my Son, my Beloved, on whom my favour rests" (Matt. 3:17, NEB). Immediately "Jesus was then led away by the Spirit into the wilderness, to be tempted by the devil" (Matt. 4:1, NEB).

This, says Douglas Rhymes,

is that experience of unity with God which was constantly both the joy and the suffering of Christ: it led Him to be driven by the Spirit into the wilderness . . . of the discovery of his real self, . . . tormented by the demons of [what would have been even for Jesus] the false self which will constantly try to hide the real in the superficial: this tormenting and yet important act of self-discovery can only be done in solitude.[13]

This is basically true for us all. We too need times of solitude, the wilderness experiences. If it was true for Simon, for Paul, for Wesley, and for our Lord, how much more for you and me. The fact is, as Thomas R. Kelly put it, "No man can look on God and live, live in his own faults, live in the shadow of the least self-deceit."[14]

It is dangerous and costly indeed to look on God in Christ, for it will first make you sick. But only as you continue looking can you become willing to receive the healing and forgiveness that makes you well.

After seeing myself in the light of God's burning, life-giving presence, the second requirement for honesty is *to accept the true and say no to the false*. In God's presence, I am able to see the truth and want it so much that I am willing to let go of the false. I am willing to exchange my way for God's way! For "what you are in God's sight, that you are, no more and no less."[15]

However young or old in years, we cannot save ourselves from the false in us. *Only in the wondrous love of the eternal Christ can I afford to be honest*. Without his acceptance, I could never stand the sight of myself as I really am. But in his presence I can truly overcome my shame and guilt and enter into a clear day where I can see more of the forever than I ever saw before.

One of our major difficulties in being honest with ourselves is distinguishing between the false self that we must hate and leave behind and the true self that we are to become. Which self is to die and which is to live? Let me share a most helpful illustration. I have used it with many persons—alcoholics with whom I was cooperating in taking the fifth step of the Alcoholics Anonymous program (to admit to God, to myself, and to another person in whom I have confidence the exact nature of my wrongs), persons with marital difficulties, youth and others who were defensively hurting and killing the very things they loved most. I have used it for many years after receiving the germinal idea for it from a lecture by the Christian pyschotherapist, Dr. Fritz Kunkel.

Which life are we to lose and which are we to find? We all want life, but seeking to save the false life means losing the authentic life!

The following symbolic diagrams are included to illustrate and interpret the costly disciplines of illumination. They are intended to make clear which self we are to lose and the resulting true self we then will find. As we talk about "denying" or "losing the self," we must strongly disclaim and reject the all too frequent misinterpretation of the teachings of Jesus and Paul that would indicate our problem is that we love our selves too much! This is a travesty on the whole emphasis of the New Testament. In Jesus' version of the two great commandments that sum up all the laws of God, he said quite plainly that we are to love God supremely and our neighbor sincerely "as you love yourself" (Matt. 22:39, TEV). Surely Jesus is saying that we cannot love our *true* selves too much! "Are you not of much more value than many sparrows, for not one sparrow falls to the ground without your Father's knowledge!"

The first symbolic diagram is a paradigm, or chart, showing the difference between living out of the HEART and the opposite kind of attempt to live out of the SHELL. The two principal teachings of Jesus this symbolic diagram interprets are (1) "If you dwell within the revelation I have brought, you are indeed my disciples; you shall know the truth, and the truth will set you free" (John 8:31–32, NEB); and (2) "If any man would come after me, let him deny himself ["leave self behind" (NEB)] and take up his cross and follow me. For whoever would save his life will lose it; and whoever loses his life for my sake and the gospel's will save it" (Mark 8:34–35, RSV).

The second Symbolic Diagram, entitled "The Divided Self," interprets our human situation so as to make more evident the source of the problem with our false selves that must be dealt with in dying to the false and rising to the true self (see Rom. 6:4–8).

Two teachings of Jesus interpreted by this paradigm are:

1. "No one can serve two masters" (Matt. 6:24);
2. "A house divided against itself cannot stand" (Mark 3:25).

The apostle Paul's classic description of the divided self, which he had experienced as "a body of death," is found in the realistic words of chapter 7 of his letter to the Romans (note especially verses 18–25). Here is a picture of what depth pyschology calls "split personality," obviously seated in our subconscious minds. All of us, to some degree at least, have experienced that about which Paul was writing when he said, "I do not understand my own actions. For I do not do what I want, but I do the very thing I hate" (v. 15, RSV), or, as the King James Version puts it, "The good that I would, I do not:

Symbolic Diagram No. 1
Understanding and Acting on the
Truth about Myself

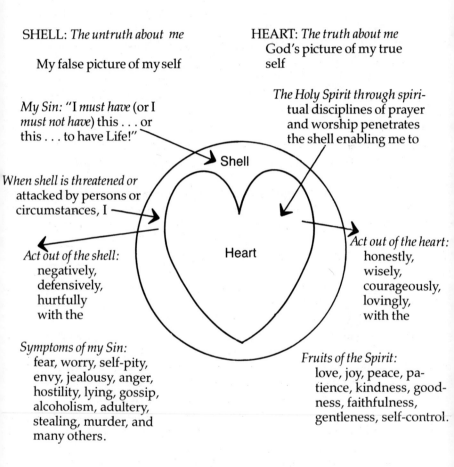

SHELL: *The untruth about me*

My false picture of my self

My Sin: "I *must have* (or I *must not have*) this . . . or this . . . to have Life!"

When shell is threatened or attacked by persons or circumstances, I

Act out of the shell:
    negatively,
    defensively,
    hurtfully
    with the

Symptoms of my Sin:
    fear, worry, self-pity,
    envy, jealousy, anger,
    hostility, lying, gossip,
    alcoholism, adultery,
    stealing, murder, and
    many others.

HEART: *The truth about me*
    God's picture of my true
    self

*The Holy Spirit through spiri-*tual disciplines of prayer and worship penetrates the shell enabling me to

Act out of the heart:
    honestly,
    wisely,
    courageously,
    lovingly,
    with the

Shell

Heart

Fruits of the Spirit:
    love, joy, peace, pa-
    tience, kindness, good-
    ness, faithfulness,
    gentleness, self-control.

Prayer and worship at their best bring:
1. *Insight* into the false and true self pictures
2. *Decision:* "NO" to the false and "YES" to the true
3. *Trust:* "I have the strength for anything through him who gives me power" (Phil. 4:13, NEB).

but the evil which I would not, that I do. . . . O wretched man that I am! who shall deliver me from the body of this death?" (vv. 19, 24).

These statements of Jesus and Paul describe the helplessness all of us feel when we are acting out of what I am calling "the shell" of inner compulsions, "the must haves" and the "must not haves" in our deepest desires, causing us to lose not only the good we seek but the true good for which we were created. The following symbolic diagram is meant to help us to discover our "Sin," which is so difficult to see and confess and which is rooted in the deep subconscious "shell":

Symbolic Diagram No. 2
The Structure of our False, Divided Self

The shell is built up by my responses since childhood to hurts and pleasures that help create a false and illusory picture of me resulting in

My Bright Side	*My Dark Side*
My "Good Self"— idealistic, noble, unselfish, doing good, "self righteous," and proud of *my* goodness! MY *OK* SELF	My "Selfish Self"— aggressive, competitive: "win at any cost;" *my* pleasures, desires, fulfillment *first!* MY *NOT OK* SELF

The Shell is made up of the two selves, both false:
1. Self-righteous—noble—idealistic, proving how good I am and expecting others to appreciate me!
2. Self-gratifying—ruthless—antagonistic, demanding others to look up to me! My desires first!

These two sides of my shell are continually fighting each other. When my bright side is winning, I feel good for the moment; when my dark side takes control, even with temporary satisfactions, I feel deeply dissatisfied with myself, driving me to more and more excesses in my attempts to win what I want. Either way, I am losing not only the life I seek to gain but the true life of loving joy and creative peace for which I am created!

Why this description of my false self and my true self is accurate is more easily understood if we realize that each of us has built around ourself the shell of a false universe—false desires, phony illusions, silly laws, which psychotherapist Dr. Fritz Kunkel calls "training formulas" carried over from childhood experiences that made us wary and self-deceitful. For instance, "I must have recognition and approval to prove I am not little and unimportant. Not just any old kind of recognition, but the approval I deserve and dream of."

"I must have plenty of money because I must not be poor, as I once was. So don't talk to me about mental, spiritual, and cultural riches. These my conscious mind as well as my deep subconscious mind simply will not accept. There is no substitute for plenty of dough!"

"I must have a certain kind of success in my position—perhaps my profession as a doctor, or a clergyperson, or something else—not the kind of success of seeing people made well or set free of injustice, but success based on my own standards or the standards of my peers."

"I must have the presence and help of my wife, my husband, or my child; therefore, I cannot accept the fact of finitude with illness, accidents, and death. Hence I am unable to overcome my grief!"

Of course, all of these desires are good within themselves, but when we make them ultimate, holding them too tightly, they become our idols or little gods. Thus, they hide or obscure the real good. This "good thing" I have made into an idol is really my Sin, though I may not recognize it as such. As Dante's definition realistically put it, in effect, "Sin is any good thing loved inordinately." *Since what I want is always good in my eyes, to want it could not be sin!* This is the reason so many Christians never confess and repent of their sin—they have never seen it. Because we so rarely see the truth about ourselves, our inner compulsions in the long run make us sick physically, mentally, and spiritually! We continue to be "consciously divided, inferior and unhappy," as William James, in his landmark book *Varieties of Religious Experience*, describes those who are only partially committed to the true God!

How great the freedom when honestly, openly, frankly, simply I stand in the presence of One who sees me as I am and reveals to me what I can be!

Symptom and Sin

The two symbolic illustrations on the preceeding pages indicate what most of us have realized when we confront the true meaning of our powerlessness to overcome negative and hurtful attitudes and acts: *we know all about our symptoms, but very little if anything about our Sin*—spelled with a capital *S* because the root of all sin is our foolish endeavor to substitute *our* good in place of God. This is *pride*, the *Hubris* as the Greeks called it: "the excessive and inordinate love of one's self, seeking to play God—the creature trying to take the place of the Creator."[16]

Yes, we are well acquainted with our little sins. We may refer to them as immaturities, imperfections, weaknesses. But all of us are conscious of the particular immaturities or habits we know are hurting us and our relations with others, threatening our health and positions. Therefore, even as Christians, when we pray, our penitence is not for our Sin but for our too-quick temper, our foolish worries the doctor says will kill us if we don't quit, our greed as we seek to make ourselves and our families "secure"—how could that be wrong? We pray for our hurt feelings and resentments at "those who don't recognize and praise our good deeds and habits"—how could that be a sin? Our self-righteousness is unseen and unrepented even though extremely hurtful to many who are repelled by our prejudice and lack of loving kindness!

How great the freedom, therefore, when in God's presence I see *beyond the symptoms to the sin—the untruth of my conscious and subconscious demands that keeps me in slavery.* My prayers of untruth are wasted breath and time. They get no further than my symptoms and are like rubbing cold cream on the red marks when I have the measles!

"I'm sorry, Lord, that I lost my temper and said such harsh and hurtful things." But deep down in my subconscious my prayer is altogether different. "I was really justified in being so harsh. It was a mean thing he did to threaten my position." Obviously losing my temper in such a situation is not my sin. My sin is the stubborn self-demands that keep me from seeing and doing the best and most constructive things in the situation, even for the enemy—what Jesus meant by "turning the other cheek," "going the second mile."[17]

"Lord, I'm sorry I worry until I'm so exhausted that I am sick and can't sleep. Please take away my worries, forgive my anxieties." I pray this consciously, but deep down I am really saying, "I am not at all sorry for idolizing my position. I am determined to protect this self-image at all costs."

"I cannot live without my Mary, my John." Here again worry and excessive grief are not my sins, but rather the demands deep down from my own desires. I am unwilling to trust the Lord of life who, if I cooperate, will bring good even out of the worst. What I need is the honest prayer of self-commitment and trust in God as I seek to live out of the "heart"—God's picture of me at my highest potential of living. This illumination from God's truth and resources gives me courage even when that which I dread the most has come upon me. This is not Pollyanna praying or wishful thinking. It is the realism of a Viktor Frankl in a Nazi concentration camp or a Paul in the Mamertine prison saying, "All joy [in the Lord] be yours. . . . The Lord is near; have no anxiety, but in everything make your requests known to God in prayer and petition with thanksgiving. Then the peace of God, which is beyond our utmost understanding, will keep guard over your hearts and your thoughts, in Christ Jesus" (Phil. 4:4, 6–7, NEB).

There is a third part of this experience of honesty—a great gift indeed! *In the presence of the living Christ, I see that the truth about me and my world is infinitely better than the half-truths and falsehoods to which I have been clinging.*

This has been the secret of every great and noble person able to be creative and free in the face of danger and seeming failure. It was Dag Hammarskjöld's secret. According to Gustaf Aulén, Hammarskjöld "fought self-centeredness in all its shapes, pursuing it to the deepest and most secret corners: 'So, once again, you chose for yourself.'"[18] This was written in 1955 during one of Hammarskjöld's attempts, as secretary general of the UN, to bring leaders of the nations together to work for peace.

> So, once again, you chose for yourself—and opened the door to chaos. The chaos you become whenever God's hand does not rest upon your head. . . .
>
> But when his attention is directed beyond and above, how strong he is, with the strength of God who is within him because he is in God. Strong and free, because his [false] self no longer exists.[19]

"His enemies included the propensity 'furtively to seek honor for yourself,' and 'a tone of voice which places you in the limelight.' 'If you go on in this way, thoughtlessly mirroring yourself in an obituary, you will soon be writing your epitaph—in two senses.'"[20]

Who has not had enough of this experience? Who would not desire to be set free if they really understood the possibilities of such freedom?

Listen to Walter Rauschenbusch (called the Prophet of the Social Awakening) describe the results of illuminating honesty before God. These words have become mine, since I took them at a crisis in my life and ministry, when the little lord self within me had come close to destroying me both physically and spiritually. One day in

January, 1947, I entered Rauschenbusch's words in my spiritual notebook. I recommend his prayer to each of you as one of the most realistic, hopeful, productive acts in which any human being may engage.

> In the castle of my soul
> Is a little postern gate,
> Whereat, when I enter,
> I am in the presence of God.
> In a moment, in the turning of a thought,
> I am where God is,
> This is a fact.
> . . . .
> All life has a meaning.
> Without asking I know:
> My desires are even now fulfilled,
> My fever is gone
> In the great quiet of God.
> My troubles are but pebbles on the road,
> My joys are like the everlasting hills.
> . . . .
> So it is when my soul steps through the postern
>   gate
> Into the presence of God.
> Big things become small, and small things
>   become great.[21]

Yes, thank God, in God's presence you have a clear day in which things once seen as big "become small, and small things become great."

Therefore when God says to me and to you, as to Simon Peter, "Lance, John, Mary, Albert, Ruth . . . do you really love me?" I am ready to answer with the ancient psalmist, with Jesus and Simon and Paul, with Dag Hammarskjöld and Walter Rauschenbusch: Yes, Lord, "search me, . . . and know my heart: try me, and know my thoughts: . . . and lead me in the way everlasting" (Psalm 139:23–24, KJV).

5

The Joyful Disciplines
of Acceptance

The Joy and Freedom of Being Accepted
and of Accepting

There is indeed no greater joy on earth than the freedom of new perspective and illumination that comes when I consciously recognize myself through authentic prayer and worship as being in the presence of God the reality we meet in Christ!

It is the freedom of coming out of the shell of the false must-haves and the joy of becoming more and more the true person that has been potential in me all along! For now I no longer struggle along false battle lines.

I do not have to have my false, twisted picture of life fulfilled! Indeed, I no longer want it fulfilled, but rather hate it as my worst enemy!

As much as I desire the presence and health of my dearest loved ones and my own physical health, I no longer feel that without these I cannot be truly alive!

My old demands look as foolish as they always were, but now I see them for what they are!

I have no compulsive need to be recognized, to be rich, to be popular, to be strong physically!

I no longer demand proof. I do not have to see and understand all the mysteries of good and evil. Like Job, I cease to ask *why* with such passionate vehemence. Rather, I ask only *how? Show* me. *Lead* me.

I can trust myself because I am trusted beyond what I deserve!

I can trust others even though I am aware of the wrong they have done or plan to do. In this trust in God and the divine purposes for us all, I can do the appropriate best thing for all in each situation.

I can love even those I do not like, yes, even those who hate me, for I trust eternal Love.

All of this is possible because I can accept what God is giving me—the priceless gift of freedom to be my authentic self.

I do not have to struggle to make myself infinitely wise, perfectly secure, but I can accept my finitude, my limitations of knowledge and strength. I know more of who I am and can be in God's sight, and the view is more wonderful than any I had imagined before.

As some of you read this, you may be tempted to shake your head or your fist! The sad and tragic fact is that so often we are lacking in this most significant insight that makes life worth living and pain and death worth meeting! "Perhaps," you may say to me, "you are indulging in a romantic fantasy. It is poetic, but unrealistic."

My answer is, "No, I am utterly serious when I say from my own experience that when we lack this illumination and its freedom, we are prevented from accepting God's most priceless gift—life at *its fullest and best.*"

It is difficult to be a real Christian today or even a person of good will and integrity. There are so many pressures and tensions, so many ambiguities of moral standards in a world where the future is filled with evil threats that all our brave self-sufficiency and vaunted technology cannot prepare us to face with confidence. We live in a world that is not immoral so much as amoral—a secular culture where there is a deep credibility gap between worship and work, belief and practice, the physical-material which is "real" and the spiritual which is "unreal." Most of us, as described in the last chapter, are split personalities. Even as professing Christians, we are like Morton Kelsey as he described himself at the beginning of his ministry as a young Episcopalian priest in a parish in California.

Kelsey had come through agnosticism having experienced "a lot of pain and destructiveness within me and around me."

> The feeble beliefs I had been given in Sunday school and church evaporated. . . . One or two of the friends of my family had been touched deeply by the reality of love, but in the company town where I was reared, they were considered unrealistic and were mocked behind their backs. . . . [Then I discovered] the trouble with most agnostics is that they were not agnostic enough. They hold on to what they want to believe and they toss aside what they find difficult and inconvenient. Real agnosticism takes away beliefs in God, meaning, morals, everything. I was left in a stormy sea with a gale raging and no anchor. . . .
>
> . . . It looked like a truly meaningless and friendless world.[1]

Then, as a teacher in a Peekskill military school, he found a small Episcopal church where he was warmly received and with a "minister [who] was actually rather intelligent." Through his help, Kelsey decided to try the church to see if Christianity really had any meaning. He entered a seminary where he "began to see that the cross and the resurrection were the center of Christianity. . . . And if [Jesus] did indeed rise again, then the best of human beings (who knew all the worst that humankind and the dull meaningless world could do) had not been snuffed out. . . . At last I could see the hand and power of God written in the fabric of human history."[2]

Kelsey was able to accept intellectually the truth of the resurrection, but, he wrote:

> I was still plagued with anxiety. I saw no hope for meaning in this war-torn world without the resurrection. However, I did not know how to bring this meaning into the center of my being. . . .
>
> . . . One of the reasons I was anxious was that I was split in two. My intellect and my worldly side had been taught that only this physical world was real. One part of me accepted unquestioningly the materialistic thesis that there is no meaning in the universe, that this physical world evolved out of blind, meaningless chaos, that

human beings are only the materialistic gene's way of reproducing itself. On the other side was my experience with spiritual reality, my actual experience of providence, grace and love, which had reduced my anxiety. Until this split could be healed I would be torn apart inside. . . . The resurrection confronted me with my inner split and gave me a way to heal it.

My anxiety and depression were abscesses on my soul which needed to be lanced.[3]

Much of this illuminating and realistic book is used by Dr. Kelsey to describe the ways by which the spiritual disciplines of prayer, worship, meditation, and contemplation allowed "the resurrected One to be constantly present" enabling him to deal with "all the evil suffered by Jesus, by my friends, and by me, . . . [to] face all the rape, pillage, war and hatred that I hear about daily, and still have hope. The resurrection reveals the ultimate nature of the universe, and the risen Christ continues to give victory over the power of evil."[4]

An Act of Ultimate Trust

Since in these pages I am sharing my own experiences in which I was enabled to accept the grace of God by faith through the disciplines of the spirit, here I will describe in greater detail a crucial hour in my growth to maturity, which further illustrates the joyful discipline of acceptance through an act of complete trust.

It was a mild November evening in a small park near Turtle Creek in Dallas, Texas, where I had gone at a crisis moment in my life. The time was 1932, the beginning of my middle year at the school of theology. The summer preceding, I had preached twice a day in what were called "Revival Meetings." This was my third summer of such work, but with one difference. As I preached, there was a big question mark before me: "How do I know there is a God like Jesus Christ? How can I be sure there was a resurrection? How can I believe in the living presence of the resurrected Christ? And how can I know that prayer is anything more than autosuggestion and self-hypnosis?"

These doubts had risen because, as a voracious reader, I had read everything I could find in all brands of philosophy and theology, including ideas such as God as the sum total of human values, and so forth. My once-assured faith with which I had begun my study and practice of the ministry was now riddled and torn with doubts. This was good for me in the end, for one who has never doubted has never really and truly believed. If I was to preach to a people with split personalities wrought by pseudo-science conflicting with the Christian faith as described above, I needed to know how to live my faith in the eternal love of the God illuminated in our Lord Jesus Christ, who raised the beloved Son from the dead and would bring all believing children from the death of self-centeredness to new life of love and joy and peace. I knew my future of life or death depended on the decision I made and the road I took.

My summer's preaching as a divided soul had ended in a near physical breakdown. I was taken home and put to bed. The doctor said, "Son, you have the highest blood pressure I have ever seen in a youth! What's the matter with you?" I knew, but I didn't tell him. After two weeks in bed, I returned to the school of theology, where, for two months, I had to rest several hours each day to keep going. That November evening I went to the little park determined to have it out. I faced realistically the three possible choices before me:

1. I could give up my faith in Christ and quit this "God talk," change my major in the university, and get out in the world and make all I could like so many. I would do good when I wanted to on my own and forget my struggles over faith in God.

2. I could go ahead and crack up, perhaps ending in a mental hospital. I knew I wasn't going to do that, nor was I giving up my intellectual belief in God revealed in Christ.

3. My only other choice was to begin living by faith, make an act of ultimate trust, and continue making it as long as I lived.

"Are you here with me, Lord Jesus, the risen Christ? Are your presence and response to my prayers real? I cannot prove or disprove it by my reason. One evidence I cannot deny: all in history or in the present whose lives I admire most have trusted in you. All who have made the greatest contributions to the welfare of humanity have believed it. If it is false, it has done more good than all the so-called 'truths' ever told. If it is false, there is no meaning and the world is a mad-house—and that I cannot believe."

In the silence of that moment, I decided to make the step of faith, an act of ultimate trust in Christ. I drew a line in the grass with the toe of my shoe. I prayed, "When I step across that line, from this moment on, O God of Christ, I am putting my life on the side of your living Presence. I am going to live by faith that you are alive and present, the Lord of the universe and my Lord, my Savior and Friend."

I stepped across the line, lifted my heart in thankful trust, and without any emotional upheaval, went back to my room and wrote down in my spiritual notebook what I was doing. From that day to this, I have acted on that faith, with continuing acts of trust. This does not mean that I have had no doubts and struggles, for I have. It does mean that I have not gone back on that basic decision to trust the real presence of the risen Christ! It also meant that in two weeks I was well and haven't had high blood pressure since!

That hour I made a landmark decision that has opened the door to my continuing acceptance of the gracious One who accepted me. Looking back, I can think of numerous other times when this decision to trust has been reaffirmed and the Holy Spirit of the mighty Christlike God has lived in and through me in ways far more wonderful than I could ever have imagined.

I am very sure, therefore, that none of us is ready for life in this frustrated and divided world as a mature person—the end result of living as a vital Christian—until we learn the gracious privilege of being accepted with all our failures and weaknesses. This is what the apostle Paul means by being "justified by faith" (Rom. 5:1–5). We will never know the overflowing, lovingly creative life until and unless we have learned to sink our roots into the flowing streams of God's grace. This can happen only through a disciplined life of prayer and worship, through intelligent, honest thinking, and through devotion and openness before God. This kind of disciplined life produces what I am calling the third great stream of living water: *acceptance*—acceptance of the perspectives that illumine us as to who we are and what life can be in the light of who God is.

These perspectives come only as we see ourselves, others, and our world through the illuminating presence of the resurrected Christ, as Jesus promised in his last message to his disciples in the upper room:

> If you love me, you will keep my commandments. And I will pray the Father, and he will give you another Counselor [the Greek word *paraclete,* meaning "one called alongside to help"] to be with you for ever, even the Spirit of truth, whom the world cannot receive, because it neither sees him nor knows him; [but] you know him, for he dwells with you, and will be in you. . . . These things I have spoken to you, while I am still with you. But the Counselor, the Holy Spirit, whom the Father will send in my name, he will teach you all things.
>
> —John 14:15–17, 25–26, RSV

The apostle Paul is saying the same thing in Colossians 1:26–27 when he declares, "The secret hidden for long ages and through many generations, but now disclosed to God's people . . . is this: Christ in you, the hope of a glory to come" (NEB).

The Holy Spirit, Christ in us, is the divine presence as the Counselor-Advocate-Comforter-Teacher who will guide us in all the costly but glorious truth about ourselves, our companions, our enemies, and all the competing and conflicting demands of the world within and without. In the light of the cross, we see the worst that human evil can do but also the most precious and powerful fact of the divine love of God for us made known by the power of the resurrection.

> Life is ever lord of Death,
> And Love can never lose its own![5]

All of this is made possible because of the Incarnation—
"The Word became flesh; he came to dwell among us,
and we saw his glory, such glory as befits the Father's
only Son, full of grace and truth" (John 1:14, NEB). Thus
the royal connection is made, writes Paul, "For if . . . we
were reconciled to God by the death of his Son, much
more, now that we are reconciled, shall we be saved by
his life" (Rom. 5:10, RSV). "Have this mind among yourselves, which is yours in Christ Jesus" (Phil. 2:5, RSV).
"Let your bearing towards one another arise out of your
life in Christ Jesus" (Phil. 2:5, NEB).

Knowing the Mind of Christ

The major question then is: *How do we find the mind of
Christ? How do we accept the help of the Counselor, the Holy
Spirit?*
In the preceding chapter, I spoke of the necessity for
disciplined attention in meditation, contemplation,
prayed-in-reading of the Bible and the writings of great
Christians, and corporate worship. *Christian prayer is attending to Christ, putting attention on him.* Here I will use a
symbolic diagram to describe the communion of our
spirits with Christ's Spirit so that we are enabled to see
our lives and the world in true perspective and accept
the gift not only of insight but of the power to become
what we see.
This symbolic diagram I am calling the Parable of the
Lens. Most of us are familiar with the process by which
the ophthalmologist or optometrist uses various
strength lenses in order to prepare eyeglasses with the
most perfect vision possible for us. The doctor tries one
lens after another until our eyes are in focus. This is the
diagram of two lenses: one the "Me Lens," the other the
"Christ Lens." As babies, we see only through the self-
centered "Me Lens." As we begin to grow and mature,
we learn to see more and more the viewpoint of others.
When we have encounters with Christ, either through
reading the New Testament account or in the words and
acts of others who have "the mind of Christ," we begin
to see a little through the "Christ Lens." As we see and

respond by an act of trusting faith, we are "born again" as we become "new creations in Christ." But this first act of "justifying faith," as Paul describes it, is but the beginning of the long pilgrimage out of our false selves into the true. At any time, we may, through pride and unbelief, refuse to look through the Christ Lens and see only the twisted and misshapen view of reality through the "Me Lens." We cannot accept the wonderful possibilities God intends for our lives until we are willing regularly to discipline our attention so that we are increasingly able to see, through the eyes of Christ, who we are and who we can become, as well as the hopeful possibilities of our families, people, and world. In order to make clear this process of seeing and accepting the perspectives of reality through Christ, the following symbolic diagram is presented:

Parable of the Lens

"Your eye is the lamp of your body; when your eye is sound [single], your whole body is full of light; but when it is not sound, your body is full of darkness" (Luke 11:34, RSV).

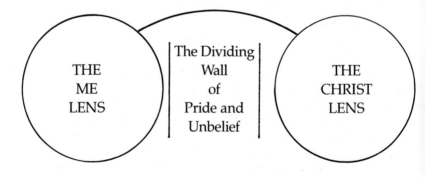

New creation in Christ begins when I see a little through the Christ Lens and accept the loving forgiveness, the direction, and power to live in the joyous freedom of the kingdom of God.

Each circle below represents the increasing ability to see through the Christ Lens a larger and larger vision of Christ and his purposes for me and the world. The first circle represents the "Me Lens" of the babe in Christ. The fourth circle, labeled "5000+," represents the perfect vision of the mature disciple who sees completely through the "Christ Lens," though as Paul wrote to the Philippians, "I have not yet reached perfection, but I press on, hoping to take hold of that for which Christ once took hold of me" (3:12, NEB). "I press on toward the goal for the prize of the upward call of God in Christ Jesus" (3:14, RSV). Our vision is *never* perfect, but we are always "going on to perfection," as John Wesley described it.[6]

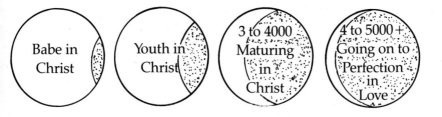

In these disciplines we accept our daily bread—forgiveness, reconciliation with God and humanity, and guidance and deliverance. All of these are summed up in the last half of the Lord's Prayer. "Father: . . . Give us day by day the food we need. Forgive us our sins, for we forgive everyone who does us wrong. And do not bring us to hard testing" (Luke 11:1, 3–4, TEV). Only when we have learned to pray this and live as we pray will the level of our ability to meet the ambiguity and tensions of life be high enough to live effectively in this world!

The tragic fact is that the meaning of vital Christian prayer and worship, even in the songs and hymns and in the other habits of devotion that once went under the name of Christian piety, is little understood and practiced today. This is nothing new, for even among the earliest Christians of Paul's day, there were those who "holding the forms of religion . . . [are] denying the power of it ["a standing denial of its reality" (NEB)] (2 Tim. 3:5, RSV). So today many have the forms of Christian prayer and worship, but are never formed by them. Why? The answer of James (4:3) is clear. "We pray but do not receive, because we pray in the wrong way to satisfy our own lusts and desires." That is, we have never surrendered our self-centered "Me Lens" through which we are praying. Let us look at what then happens.

When Christian Prayer and Worship Are Not Fully Christian

There are at least *five ways professing Christians pray that may be religious but are not Christian in the sense of keeping the lenses of our minds and hearts in focus with the "Mind of Christ."* As such, our prayers are inadequate to provide our starving souls with the bread of life and the ability to forgive as we are forgiven, to stand the tests of temptation as we are led into the right paths, and to be delivered from the evils that threaten us within and without. Our prayers and other forms of devotion are therefore deceptive and illusory. They may even be destructive! For, at best, they are based on partial truth and may cause us to miss the gracious truth that makes us whole and upon which our fullest life depends!

As a result of these inadequate and false ways of praying, millions who still profess Christian beliefs, even many ordained ministers, have quit praying except as a last resort. Then they may turn in their desperation to the unknown God who *might* be there!

1. *The first of these five ways is the childish (not childlike)*

approach to prayer as "Gimme," "Help me get what I want, the good that I see and must have."

We are like the little boy who, when his pastor asked him, "Sonny, do you say your prayers every night," answered, "No sir, some nights I don't want anything!"

The idea is: when there is a need I can't meet, I beg God and God comes running, ready to pull my little red wagon wherever I want it to go! Bishop A. T. Robinson refers to this as prayer to "the God of the gaps"; but the gaps are mostly closed. For example, much of the time we no longer need God when we are sick, for there is penicillin or surgery, the doctor, and medicine! And for protection, we have safety belts and common sense! What more does a liberated man or woman need?

2. *The second of these approaches to prayer might be called The Adolescent Level—the reasons for* not *praying.* Realizing how foolish our childish prayer was, we may give up prayer as unscientific, superstitious magic. Not seeing enough through the "Christ Lens," we miss the rich and glorious meaning of prayer and worship as loving and adoring attention to the One whose love "surpasses all understanding" and as the joyous acceptance of life to the full in the kingdom of God for which we are made. We are strangely like that boy hero, Mark Twain's Huckleberry Finn, who sadly confessed the failure of his prayers:

> Miss Watson she took me in the closet and prayed, but nothing come of it. She told me to pray every day, and whatever I asked for I would get it. But it warn't so. I tried it. Once I got a fish-line, but no hooks. . . . I tried for the hooks three or four times, but somehow I couldn't make it work. By and by, one day, I asked Miss Watson to try for me, but she said I was a fool. She never told me why, and I couldn't make it out no way.
>
> I set down one time back in the woods, and had a long think about it. I says to myself, if a body can get anything they pray for, why don't Deacon Winn get back the money he lost on pork? Why can't the widow get back her silver snuff-box that was stole? Why can't Miss Watson fat up? No, says I to myself, there ain't nothing in it.[7]

Many who think of themselves as very "scientific" have reached this simplistic and completely unscientific conclusion, "No, there ain't nothing in it!"

3. *The third of these inadequate approaches to prayer is the immature prayer of purely human psychological self-adjustment*—the prayers of positive thinking that bring peace of mind. If we know just the right words and methods of meditation and bio-feedback, we are told, we can receive health and wealth and life to the full. Now, surely, positive thinking is infinitely better than negative thinking and could be and very well is a part of Christian prayer at its best.

We can all learn ways of meditation from the Eastern religions that can be ways of looking through the "Christ Lens" and loving the priceless possibilities of good God has for us. But if this is all we have in our spirituality, we are indeed a million miles from Christian prayer and worship at their best. The sad fact is that many people are depending on the "bootstrap" religion of psychology with hundreds of books that tell us how we can manage our thoughts in order to find the self-fulfillment we want in our own way and on our own terms.

Professor Paul Vitz of New York University has written a much-needed book entitled, *Psychology as Religion—The Cult of Self-Worship*. The book describes the utter inadequacy of the purely psychological approach to religion, as he discovered after forty years of depending on it![8] The result of this "cult of self-worship," the me-centered approach to our quest for the fullest life, is also described by psychiatrist Aaron Stern in his rather startling book *ME: The Narcissistic American*, in which he warns that unless we in America overcome our narcissism, that is, our me-first, self-centeredness, we will not be able to make the necessary sacrifices of loving cooperation required for our survival as a free society.[9] The way to destruction is broad and seems to be easy, but in the end is the hardest and infinitely most costly way: it is the self-centered way in which I try to play God. Even in my prayer, it won't work. Using God in psychological self-adjustment leads to confusion and futility. As the bit of doggerel puts it:

> The centipede was happy quite,
>   Until the frog for fun, said,
> "Pray, which leg comes after which?"
> This threw him into such a pitch
> He fell distracted in the ditch,
>   Forgetting how to run!

4. *The fourth kind of inadequate praying might be called simply the prayer of social action—to do good is to pray.* The best prayer is actually going out to remove injustice, to release the oppressed, to heal and restore the hurt and wounded, and to meet great human need. There is much to be said for this kind of praying. It is certainly to be preferred to the false or inadequate praying of the first three levels. Indeed, the highest level of Christian prayer, to be described in chapter 6, is the disciplined and intentional prayer of caring love. The chief difficulty, and to my mind and experience an insufferable one, is that prayer primarily as "doing good to others" is without adequate foundations of joyful acceptance of the divine love that motivates and inspires my social action. I am going out as one little, self-sufficient person, joining others who have the same ideals, but without the perspective of who we are or why we should care.

With this approach, we have no deep roots that can supply us with the proper insights, the necessary patience, and above all, the love needed when the going is rough. For our concerned action *is* going to be rebuffed and unappreciated. If we continue, we will be faced with the cross or its equivalent. Then, as countless persons have done, we may give up our idealism and seek to escape. Or we may join the anarchists who would blindly destroy what they cannot change. As self-sufficient persons depending solely on our own resources and the help of our fellows, our "prayer of action" is soon likely to be empty and then discarded as the way gets rougher.

5. *The fifth and probably most illusory of the inadequate*

ways we as Christians often pray is prayer purely as intellectual-analyzing, thinking about God and prayer, trying to get just the right words to say. As one dear person said to me when I counseled her in her problems and suggested she pray using the insights she had found: "Oh, but Dr. Lance, I don't know the words to use!" As if that had anything to do with her deepest and best praying!

Jesus spoke to this kind of prayers: "In praying do not heap up empty phrases as the Gentiles do; for they think that they will be heard for their many words" (Matt. 6:7, RSV).

Henri J. M. Nouwen declares that this is one of the principal reasons many ministers and other sincere Christians

> pray very little or not at all. They realize that they should not forget to pray, that they should take time to pray, and that prayer should be a priority in their lives. But all these "shoulds" do not have the power to carry them over the enormous obstacle of their activitism. There is always one more phone call, one more letter, one more visit, one more meeting. . . . Together these form an insurmountable pile of activities. . . . [They may] think of prayer primarily as an activity of the mind that involves above all else our intellectual capacities. This prejudice reduces prayer to speaking with God or thinking about God. . . . Thinking about God becomes one more demanding burden. . . . The crisis of our prayer life is that our mind may be filled with ideas of God while our heart remains far from him. *Real prayer comes from the heart.*[10]

Yes, real prayer that brings joyous acceptance of the bread and water of life comes from the heart. The heart is the symbol we use for our deepest selves, including our physical, intellectual, volitional, and moral selves. "If with all your hearts you truly seek me, you shall ever truly find me, thus says the Lord."

How Then Do We Pray and Worship from the Heart?

That is the key question to which we now address ourselves.

The fact is that on any of these five levels we lose the deep meaning and power of Christian prayer: the *perspective* that brings *illumination* that leads to *acceptance* and *caring involvement*.

These are all key words to describe the life-giving results of praying in a genuinely Christlike manner. When we tap the living water of *acceptance,* several valuable experiences result.

We find the *wisdom* and *courage* to accept "the food we need for today," which includes not only a *sense of purpose,* but the health and strength of mind and body to fulfill it.

We accept ourselves as forgiven so that we no longer need carry with us the burden of guilt over past failures and sins. This means also that because we "accept our acceptance" in the forgiving love of God, we can accept and forgive ourselves—and that is one of the hardest of all accomplishments. Then and then only can we truly *forgive others.*

Still another part of this "bread for today" is the acceptance of the *guidance* we so greatly need in order to make choices leading to the good in even the worst times.

Thus we can accept the *deliverance* from the evils and temptations that threaten to test us beyond our ability to overcome or to endure.

As we think of each of these kinds of acceptance that mark Christian prayer at its authentic best, it is obvious that each has been associated too often with what might be called "magical hocus-pocus"—or just plain superstition! However, the true meaning of forgiveness, guidance, and deliverance for one who has at last said no to the false life and yes to the true life as the Spirit reveals it is not superstition but the most intelligent realism! For it will bring life over death, hope out of despair, joy out of sadness, and love over hate. To understand these meanings, let us consider each of these four last phrases of the prayer of Jesus.

Give Us This Day Our Daily Bread

It is obvious, or ought to be, that before we can give bread to others, we must be fed. We must first accept our own creatureliness, recognizing our humble dependence not only on our fellow-man but primarily on the Source and Giver of life. "He is," says Jacopone de Todi, "the grand donatore, Pastor and Pasture of the soul."

In these days of space travel, we recognize how completely we depend on each other and even more on the rich resources and laws of our physical and personal universe. So with faith we pray, "Give us this day our daily bread."

To pray thus is not to beg but to accept. God the Creator to whom Jesus prayed does not want beggars but offspring. Beggars wheedle and whimper. Offspring ask and receive, according to their deepest needs. Artists have painted different kinds of praying hands. Albrecht Dürer painted uplifted hands of adoration and blessing. Another artist painted open hands receiving gifts from the Creator of life. Both pictures are valid: hands that express the living adoration of reverence, yielded, submitting to a greater wisdom and love than ours, and also hands that express the open receptiveness of trusting hearts that eagerly receive all God has to give. "Ask, seek, knock, and you *will* receive" was Jesus' admonition (Luke 11:9–10, AUTHOR PARAPHRASE). But ask not as abject worms in the dust, cowering slaves before a hard master. No, you are to ask, seek, and knock with persistence as offspring of God, who knows your needs better than you know them. Unworthy? Yes, but made worthy by being called to the life of offspring (cf. Gal. 4:6–7.)

Jesus taught us to ask for and accept the bread for today's needs and when tomorrow comes, there will be bread enough for that day too!

God's bread is mostly plain bread—not some purely spiritual substance for ethereal souls, but substantial bread for the whole persons that we are. We can, under some circumstances, live for days without physical bread, but our fullest life comes when we have bread for all our needs: physical, mental, and spiritual, including our brothers and sisters' needs as well. Indeed, it is bread for our common life, its toils and trials, its joy and laughter, its griefs and troubles, its hurts and surprises, including each painful step of self-knowledge, every opportunity to love and to give. In all of these, God's bread is given and those who accept are fed! Surely this is what Jesus meant when he said, "I am the bread of life, he that eats of the bread I shall give him shall never hunger, and he that drinks of the water I shall give him shall never thirst!" (John 6:35, AUTHOR PARAPHRASE).

Lest these words be dismissed as abstract and ethereal, let me illustrate the difference Christian prayer and worship, the acceptance of that bread and water of life, make. Such acceptance is the opposite of the proud rejection or the equally proud taking by force what I want. It is acceptance in trust of the vision and strength, the hope and help needed for this day and all the days to come, not for ourselves only but for everyone else as well.

My daughter Jeanne has given me the privilege of sharing her experiences at two stages of her life. The first was at age thirty-six when she found herself literally starving to death for this "plain bread of life." This was true even though she had grown up in a Christian home and church, where she had been taught since infancy the meanings of the Christian faith. She is an unusually gifted person with a superb soprano voice and excellent skills as an organist, pianist, and choral director. She is a good thinker and teacher with a striking, lovable personality. Let me quote directly from her own account of the crisis in which she began to take "bread for daily needs," as she had never been able to do before.

For most of my thirty-six years God's living presence has been very real in my life. There have been dry spells of months in which I have felt very alienated from God. Each time this has happened, my return has been a marvelously joyous experience.

Finally one winter, I discovered the source of these

periods of alienation. I have conscientiously and caringly tried to do "God's will," to be the person God wanted me to be, to use to the full *all* the gifts God has given me.

Most of the time, it seemed fairly obvious what God would have me do, and I seemed to be extremely successful in carrying out these goals. I worked hard and was never satisfied until I had given my best to achieve success. All the while my self-confidence was blossoming, and I felt that undoubtedly I could accomplish *well* whatever *I* might set out to do.

As these next years progressed, the instant successes I had known became much harder to achieve, and life wasn't handing out the bouquets I was used to. The dry spells were more frequent, and I became a very angry young woman, fighting myself and the circumstances of my life. I was furious because it was so increasingly evident that I was *not* fulfilling *my* own plan of life which I identified as "God's plans" for me. Here I was, the "Great Jeanne"—a modern success story capable of such exciting things—struggling to take care of a huge house that only got dirty again the minute it was cleaned, facing an endless succession of meals to cook, dishes to wash, crying, fighting children, and a husband with needs and a ministry to be shared. Yes, I was involved in music and youth and teaching, but so very little of it was even *touching* the resources I felt were stored within me. *I was failing God and everyone, and I was furious and sick—physically and spiritually sick.*

The crisis came when she painfully realized that she could not do both her music and her home in the perfect way she wanted to do them. She was torn between her responsibilities as mother and wife and her desires for self-fulfillment as a musician. Her "must-haves" were tearing her apart even while she continued praying and asking God for help. While she rebelled at her impossible situation, it became worse.

Finally I faced the fact that I was heading straight into physical and emotional disaster. All the strong willpower and self-sufficiency and even my prayers to God for strength were not going to pull me through this time! I had reached the very *bottom* of my *own* resources. I had never been here before. In desperation I was reading some devotional material. Here were the words I had heard so often and had always found to be distasteful: *"submit"*—"Submit *all* your life! *All your plans!* And *then accept life as it comes!"*

I had rejected this approach before because it had always seemed to be a *cop-out*! It appeared to be just a good excuse to give up! Surely, I felt, God expects more of me! And so with *my* strong will I had never really completely submitted myself to God's will.

Now at last I was ready. I really had no choice, except going under completely.

I had been using the guitar to teach old and new folk songs to the youth in my church. On this day of my saying yes to God's will for me, whatever it might involve, I wrote some new words to the old spiritual, "Lonesome Valley." I knew from experience the truth of the first stanza.

> Jesus walked this lonesome valley
> . . . .
> Nobody else could walk it for
>   him.

Now, as a means to my acceptance and commitment, I added two more.

> There is hope within my valley.
> There is hope for my despair.
> No more alone within my valley.
> Jesus is with me and he cares.

> Jesus, I submit my future
> With its worries and its fears.
> Now as I walk along my valley
> Hope for life and strength appears.
> Now Jesus walks beside me here.

One result of my complete submission to God was that I began to find the insights I so desperately needed—the "third viewpoint!" I looked at my life from God's perspective and was amazed to see so many meaningful, exciting ways to use my talents. Actually I had been aware of many of these possibilities before but had impatiently rejected them because they seemed inferior to the "great" plans I knew God had for me.

Now I see that these "great" plans in and of themselves are quite shallow. Someday, I may yet carry out some of these ideas, but how much more exciting it is to live fully and wholly in the real world in which I actually find myself today.

Jeanne began to walk in her new life of submission and acceptance of herself, her family, her musical gifts, and her ability to lead others.

On one particularly difficult day, these words came to her, describing this new perspective on life:

What Is Life?

It is the process of being hurt and of hurting, of forgiving and of being forgiven, of loving and of being loved.

It contains much pain and frustration. . . . It seems impossible.

It contains God . . . and the grace of his presence.

It contains victory and an absurd triumph over all odds and against all reason.

It continues to wring and twist our private little hopes and dreams until they are ragged, torn, and meaningless.

Finally, when all seems wrecked and beyond repair, it throws us into a new perspective and a new vision . . .

IF——We have eyes to see.

(If we cannot see, then there is no more life . . . WE ARE DEAD . . . even if our bodies continue to function for awhile longer.)

Side by side with disaster then, life brings peace and an unbelievable strength.

I submit myself, O God, to life . . . to the LIFE you give.

Commenting on her new freedom and strength, she wrote, "This was what my new life was all about. The disaster was gone. The same situations were present, but I had a whole new creative approach. I found new ways of using my talents and a perspective on what I was already doing that transformed everything."

Fourteen years later, she has multiplied evidences of this priceless fact. Recently she shared with me some of the shattering experiences that she and her husband were facing as pastor and wife in their church work and that she was encountering as a school music teacher. She had reached another crisis stage at the age of fifty. She offered to permit me to quote from "Jeanne's Journal," as she calls it, some of the ways by which she has been saved "from the Pit" of discouragement and despair. Here are a few paragraphs from her journal:

> Wednesday: It occurs to me at this time when I should be sleeping that the meaning of life is to be found in one's ability to take all the splintered pieces of existence and put them together in such a way that they work—that successful experiences are finally produced. . . . So, if and when some of the good things I have now and enjoy and think essential become broken and blown away in the winds of life, I will remember all the times *I have taken broken pieces and [by God's help] made a new life!*

> Sunday Night
> "He redeems my life from the pit and crowns me with love and compassion. He satisfies my desires with good things, so that my youth is renewed like the eagle's" (Psalm 103:4–5, NIV).
> O God, you have redeemed me from the Pit over and over this past wild year! And yet again my life hovers over new pits. Still, I feel crowned with your love and compassion—encircling and encompassing my being. I see over and over how good things abound in my life. So many good things that my deepest desires are satisfied.

> Tuesday: A new trauma! I feel helpless. The great successful perfectionist is falling apart!
> Obviously, I've got to get the "great successful per-

fectionist" out of the way. She is the source of this sick
pride that can't face rejection and apparent failure.

I know what is needed. Let go of your *must haves*. Let
go of your *can't haves*. Praise the Lord for what you *do
have* and take your "daily bread" as it comes without
jealousy or resentment. Why are you here on earth anyway! To be glorified and exalted? or to love and serve?

I open all the windows and doors of my soul to you, O
God. Fill me with serenity and wholeness and use me
until I am so centered upon your love and life that it is no
longer I who lives but Christ who lives in me.

Here indeed we see in her life the joyful discipline of
acceptance. She learned as we must learn, that *she could
not receive unless she were willing to give,* and not under her
conditions but God's. She learned to pray, "Our Father
. . . your will be done. . . . Give us day by day the food we
need."

OUR Father . . . OUR Bread

Notice that it is *Our Father* to whom we pray, "Give *us*
our daily bread." She, like so many of us who have
prayed the Lord's Prayer all our lives, had prayed too often for "*my* bread, the right and power to fulfill myself."
"Surely this is *my* right, is it not, to do *my* thing?" But if
we pray in truth, we soon discover that "*my* thing" is
really "*our* thing" and the ability to fulfill *myself* comes as
I submit my self-fulfillment to the larger fulfillment of
God's way for all who are involved in my situation. For
all of us, like Jeanne, are related to others.

Indeed, the whole tenor of Jesus' life and teaching indicates his conviction that all who are not interested in
and involved with others in a concern for the daily bread
of those others cannot accept the bread they themselves
need. "I was hungered and you gave me nothing to
eat. . . . Depart from me; I never knew you." (Matt.
25:42, AUTHOR PARAPHRASE).

Indeed, God's bread is given to us in large bundles,
too much for our own consumption alone. If we try to
keep it for ourselves, we get fat and sick, as happens to

so many today, physically and spiritually. This approach to "*my* bread" leads to boredom, hatred, and wrong relationships with others.

For instance, it is tragic when ordained ministers lose their bread—their acceptance of the purpose God has for them and their submission to the greater good—because they are so desperately concerned to get their own self-fulfillment, to find their place and position, to be recognized. As a result, when the people come to worship, they look up to the ministers and are not fed. It is equally tragic for parents and other adults to give their children "a stone when they ask for bread or a serpent when they ask for fish," as Jesus put it. If they don't have any bread for themselves, how can they give it to their children? Like Jeanne, they may have the words of the good news, but they have not accepted the relationship that would enable them to be free, creative, and loving. We cannot give the bread of life to anyone else when we haven't accepted it and, like Jeanne, are literally starving to death for lack of it.

This is not only true in our family relationships, but in our wider relationships in the church, in the communities, and in the world where we live. We will certainly lose our own bread if we continue unconcerned with bread for all of the children of God—in East St. Louis, in Dallas, in Peoria, in Chicago, in Mississippi, in South America, in Ethiopia, in India, or wherever they starve physically or spiritually. This is an immutable law in our human relatedness. We are economically, geographically, and spiritually *one* people—God's children, and we all need bread. *Give us this day our daily bread.*

Forgive Us as We Forgive Those Who Have Wronged Us

Christian prayer and worship are *the acceptance of forgiveness with the corresponding ability to forgive others.* Indeed, we cannot accept ourselves as forgiven unless we accept others and forgive them. This is also an immutable law of personal health and life.

Here again, forgiveness of both kinds is the acceptance of a gift. We cannot, with our own limited abilities, correct the disorder and heal the hurts, hates, and self-ishness or bridge the gaps cut in the tender flesh of our own hearts or of our families, our cities, our nation, or our world. When I am hurt and stepped on, my security and rights threatened or removed, and I stand alone facing the world as my enemy, I can do one of three things.

I can give up and cravenly crawl into my shell of bitterness, protecting myself as best I can while I hide, hate, and finally die. Many people choose this way as various kinds of mental illness attest, including addiction to drugs, alcohol, money, or a craving for power.

If I do not withdraw and escape from the rejections and indignities that come to me, I may strike out at others in revenge. To get out my hostilities may be healthier for me at the moment, but to do so as a way of life creates a growing circle of hatred and hostilities. All youths who leave home because of lack of acceptance do so partially to get revenge on those who may really care for them. If the feeling of being unwanted and "put down" is strong enough, these youths may actually enter upon a life of crime in order to vent their hostilities on family, teachers, and the uncaring world!

This motive of "standing up for my rights," "getting even," "showing them I'm not the inferior person they think I am" is the basis for *personal* wars of every kind. In the same manner, group or racial feelings of insecurity and inferiority result in class, racial, and national wars. The rapid growth of the Nazi party, shown so vividly in *The Rise of the Third Reich* by William Shirer, is certainly traceable to this revenge—"We'll show the rest of the world what a great people we are." This is surely the mood of many black and white militants who desire revenge more than reconstruction. But though our hatred is turned toward great evils and injustices, the way of hostility and revenge is, in the end, more destructive than constructive. Like Don Quixote, we go out fighting windmills of evil and attacking the injustices about us with righteous feelings, but without the spirit of Christ-like love, we return with our own sword of life bruised and broken.

A minister may preach "prophetic sermons" in the

name of fighting evils. But when these messages express more of the hostilities of the preacher than genuine concern for the hurts of others, they will always fail.

The unforgiving, merciless spirit, no matter whether in parent, teacher, pastor, bishop, reformer, or just plain citizen, cannot bring the healing, reconciling spirit of Christ into any situation. This is true no matter how just the cause or how unjust the evils that are attacked. This merciless spirit is the source of the unrecognized but potent anarchy, right or left, in those who would destroy the church or the state or the university or the home because they have been hurt by the system or by some authority figure in it. In this spirit, their tactics are often, in the end, self-defeating. The right against wrongs and injustice should never be abandoned; but without forgiving acceptance the only possibility is to destroy the enemy, even if it means destroying oneself and, like ancient Samson, pulling the temple down not only on our own heads but on everybody around us! This blind revolution ends in nihilism. It is a million miles away from anything constructive, from any kind of creative revolution that embraces the hurt and wounded, that works effectively with others for changes to prevent the continuation of the injustice.

Then there is the *way of forgiveness*. Instead of destroying the enemy, I am ready to treat the enemy as a friend, not giving up or over to evil, but in many cases breaking down the walls between us and helping the enemy to work with me for good. Even when this happy reconciliation is rejected by the other person, I am still able to accept the suffering involved without bitterness! This truth holds good in group as well as personal situations. Sometimes I cannot change it myself. If my witness in opposition to the evils, however costly, is to be constructive, it will require a genuinely forgiving approach.

Another fact needs to be recognized. *One who does not accept oneself as forgiven cannot forgive,* and *one who does not forgive cannot accept oneself as forgiven!* This impasse can be met only by the love of Christ, who forgives us before we ask. No matter how we fight and struggle with all the hurt we do for ourselves and others, Christ never treats us as the enemy! He may let me suffer the results of my sin, but he always goes with me to the "pig pen" where I find myself hungry and forsaken; and, when I let him, he forgives and leads me back to life! Consider the words of Jesus to the poor, bitter paralytic, blaming and hating God and himself for his illness, as he was let down from the roof top in the presence of Jesus. "Your sins are forgiven. . . . Rise, take up your bed and go home" (Matt. 9:2, 7, RSV).

Or consider the soldiers and the mob who took out their hostilities toward life and others on the innocent and loving Jesus as they nailed him to the cross. Neither had they asked for forgiveness, but they heard his words spoken from the depths of his own suffering, "Father, forgive them; for they know not what they do" (Luke 23:34, RSV).

This gift is what John Wesley and others have called "prevenient grace"—God's gracious love that is there for me before I ask for it! But to be mine and to be given to others, I must accept it.[11]

The precious gift of God's acceptance and forgiveness enabling me to accept and to forgive myself has been given to me over and over in the crisis times when my self-assurance and self-dependence were badly shaken. Suddenly seeing oneself as self-centered and hurting one's own loved ones through self-centeredness is the costliest of all revelations! No doubt it is one of the bitterest pills anyone is called to take. Perhaps it is even more costly than seeing and accepting one's hurtful failures and immaturities in one's own vocation or social life. Many times I have needed desperately the medicine of self-acceptance and forgiveness in both worlds.

I have told the story of the way I came to begin a new discipline of taking the first period each morning in my study to read, think, and verbalize my failures and the way out of them. This was the result of a different kind of crisis through the words of my layman friend who pointed up that, with all my good intentions, I had become so busy "building a church" I did not have time to care very much for the people as persons. That really hurt. The words pierced my shell and showed me how inadequate and sick of false self-love I really was. I truly *did* care for persons, but I was letting my "must-haves" in regard to building the physical church get in my way. I recall this experience because it points up the fact that without the accepting love of God, such a costly self-revelation through the frankness of a friend would have left me in utter despair. I might have left the ministry right then. The one saving element was what the apostle Paul calls, "the justifying faith" in Christ who, when I accepted his forgiveness and acceptance, gave me the power to accept and forgive myself. Then came the even greater gift of wisdom and courage to begin the disciplines that would let me act more and more in "the maturity of a man in Christ." As Paul puts it so well:

> I do not claim that I have already succeeded or have already become perfect. I keep striving to win the prize for which Christ Jesus has already won me to himself. Of course, my brothers, I really do not think that I have already won it [maturity in Christ]; the one thing I do, however, is to forget what is behind me and do my best to reach what is ahead. So I run straight toward the goal in order to win the prize.
>
> —Phil. 3:12–14, TEV

Often during these years since I began this honest kind of praying, I have needed to accept my acceptance and to understand my sickness and to start again toward God's goal for me. Most of us, if we are truly honest, will need to say many times in effect: Here I stand, one who constantly falls short and knows it, often blinded by prejudice, sick of false self-love, capable of hatred and envy, even of fury and violence, one who could have done more for others and for my own better self and did not. I thought I was strong and turned out to be weak, having hurt others and myself. But here I stand, not an outcast or outsider, or counted as a stranger and foreigner, but facing the tremendous fact that I am still a child of God.

What can I do but be glad and accept it all with joy and thanksgiving and then turn to accept and forgive others who are hurting from the betrayal by their false selves and are full of fear, guilt, hostility, and failure. So now I pray, "God, I accept your forgiveness which I could not possibly deserve even as I accept the grace to forgive others who could not possibly deserve it. I give forgiveness to them. Whether or not they accept it is not my responsibility!" What freedom and creativity are mine with this simple life acceptance!

> What wondrous love is this, O my soul, O my soul,
> What wondrous love is this, O my soul!
> What wondrous love is this that caused the Lord of
>   bliss
> To bear the dreadful curse for my soul, for my soul,
> To bear the dreadful curse for my soul.[12]

The discipline of thoughtful, prayerful attention to and acceptance of this ever-present giving-love at the heart of the Eternal is the genesis and the fulfillment of life at its best.

Lead Us—Not into Temptation and Do Not Bring Us to the Test

The emphasis here is on the first two words *lead us*, rather than on the word *not*. Christian prayer and worship are the acceptance of guidance—the light and leading I need along the perilous way I must go. "*Lead us*—not into temptation—keep us from the tests we are unable to meet.

This is not begging for light and waiting till it comes, but taking one step at a time on faith in the light I have, and the light I see shows the way for another and another and still another step!

As a boy listening to my father, I shall not forget one sermon on the text, "The path of the just is as the shining light, that shineth more and more unto the perfect day" (Prov. 4:18, KJV). He told the story of a dark night in which his own father took him through a dark path in the woods with only the dim light of a kerosene lantern to show the way. His boyish fright was removed as they went deeper into the darkness. His father talked with him reassuringly and showed him that with each step they took, the lantern lighted the way for the next step.

Obviously this prayer of acceptance of the light for each step is not for the self-willed persons who demand their own way. Nor is it for the would-be beginner who has not yet taken the first step and learned to accept the gifts of the Spirit. It is for the committed follower of Christ, whether taking the second or third or three-thousandth step, because this person is already surrendered to the higher will and now *accepts* the insights and leadings necessary. This is not a magical guidance, as some religious people claim, making thought and struggle unnecessary, but it is enough light to keep going even in the darkest hour. "My times are in your hands" as the old hymn puts it. "I am always aware of your presence; when you hold me, I cannot fall," cried the psalmist (Psalm 16:8, CHAMBERLAIN).

I suppose this is the reason for the secularist's greatest skepticism about prayer. Studying history, one reads about many persons, even well-known Christians such as John Calvin, who in the name of Christ burned Servetus at the stake. Servetus, though a good man and a faithful Christian, had differed with Calvin in a crucial part of his theology. Calvin had him burned because he believed that it was Christ's will guiding him to do it! How often this has happened. Many good men and women, believing they were doing right, have prayed for guidance and, in the name of Christ, have done many foolish, hurtful things. Knowing this, many honest, secular-minded persons have quit praying and abandoned worship.

What they overlook is the world of difference between the one who prays, "Show me your will and I will *then* decide whether or not I want to do it," and the one who prays, "Your will be done, no matter the cost to me—*only show me the way*." Of course mistakes will be made, but the one least likely to make such mistakes is the person who is utterly willing and open to the truth of highest reality, or who, if mistakes are made, is the most likely to see them and correct them before too much harm is done!

The acceptance of being led by a wisdom and love greater than ours is too great a gift to be ignored or denied because of misunderstanding and misuse. Our highest human privilege is to pray with John Henry Cardinal Newman:

> Lead, Kindly Light, amid the encircling gloom,
> Lead Thou me on!
> The night is dark, and I am far from home,—
> Lead Thou me on!
> Keep Thou my feet; I do not ask to see
> The distant scene,—one step enough for me.
>
> I was not ever thus, nor prayed that Thou
>   Shouldst lead me on.
> I loved to choose and see my path; but now
>   Lead Thou me on!
> I loved the garish day, and, spite of fears
>   Pride ruled my will: remember not past years.
>
> So long Thy power hath blest me, sure it still
>   Will lead me on
> O'er moor and fen, o'er crag and torrent, till
>   The night is gone;
> And with the morn those angel faces smile
> Which I have loved long since, and lost awhile.[13]

How this leading comes is a mystery, but that it comes is a blessed and irrefutable fact of my own and many other persons' experience.

When Divine Guidance Is Authentic

Looking back over the way I have come, I am sure that my own call to the ministry was one of these experiences. Of course, I cannot prove this, but I believe definitely that my mind was being guided by a Mind greater than my own in the conviction arrived at on Easter Sunday, 1929. I was convinced then, as now, that the greatest needs of the personal world and my abilities to help meet them all pointed in the direction of the pastoral ministry. No doubt this experience that I call guidance or leading may be partly explained as the result of the example and influence of my parents, of Dr. J. W. Hunt, the father of my wife Elizabeth and the founder and president of McMurry College, where we were both in school, and of others. But the results in my life of a growing dedication to Christ in spite of all my stumbling failures point to the deeper influence of the Spirit then and in the years since. My shell of false self-demands has had to be pierced and crushed many times in costly tests; but in every one of these crushing times, I have made new surrenders of my false self in order to become more of my true self as I am led to believe God intends me to be. I am learning to get the "Me Lens" more and more in focus with the "Christ Lens" as I accept the real truth about me and my world.

If this is superstition and falsehood, make the most of it! It has certainly produced what, to me, is life filled with joyous creativity and love. It is to me *truth*, indeed the evidence of life! In submission and acceptance of the loving purposes that God has for me, I *have* been *guided* into the positive best ways to meet these "shell-crushing" experiences. *The most creative periods of my life have followed, without exception, the most costly experiences of failure, or of opposition and injustice.*

One "shell-crushing" experience during which I found genuine guidance and help in my disciplines of reading, prayer, and meditation was the result of a real disappointment in my relationships with some of my fellow pastors. Unknown to me there were some misunderstandings of me and my "ambitions," and, as a result, some false and unjust accusations were made by some of my fellow pastors. I was totally unprepared for the coldness and hostility I felt directed toward me in a very critical situation in my ministry. The loss to me was not the hardest blow by any means—though naturally I was disappointed. The greatest disappointment was in my brothers' misunderstanding of my motives, the accusations about my position and actions that all who really knew me agreed were unjust and uncalled for.

That night, angry and indignant over the injustice of

the accusations, I had to make a new surrender. I submitted myself again to Christ and his purposes for me. In the struggle that followed, I wrote this very honest prayer:

> A terrific day and week . . . Lord, wherein *I* am wrong, *forgive me*. Wherein I have been wrongfully opposed and accused, *forgive those who did it*. Grant me, O Holy Spirit of God, the power to rise above this disappointment and win through to a greater and stronger love and trust. Help me to love _____ and all of his followers. They did not really understand what they were doing. . . . Grant me the power to rejoice in your victories and to trust in your grace. *Amen.*

Three days later I was still wrestling with the little demons of self-will in my subconscious mind. I prayed:

> O Holy Spirit, enter the open doors of my heart and teach me all things I need to know about myself, my motives, my actions. Teach me to serve you . . . with one simple glad trust. Fill me with peace that all these confusions shall go and I shall be one with you! One in purpose, love, and power—your greatness infused in my littleness—your wisdom into my ignorance—your love into my self-centeredness—your mercy into my needy soul. O Holy Spirit, enter into my heart and teach me.

In the following days, I continued to wrestle with the hurts that had struck deep at my false self-image. Then one morning, my reading brought me precisely to the words I needed. They were from François de Fénelon. Through the words describing his experience, the Spirit brought me the very guidance I required.

> O man of little faith! What are you afraid of? Let God act. Abandon yourself to Him. You will suffer, but you will suffer with love, peace and consolation. . . . You will sacrifice your liberty freely and you will enter into a

new liberty unknown to the world, in which you do nothing except for love. . . .

The more we love Him, the more we love also all that He makes us to do. It is this love that consoles us in our losses, which softens our crosses for us, which detaches us from all that is dangerous to love, which preserves us from a thousand poisons.[14]

To be *"preserved from a thousand poisons!"* I know this was *true* guidance because this is what began to happen to me. I was preserved from the poisons of embitterment, jealousy, hatred, and revenge, any one of which would have consumed me. By the end of the month, I had won the victory and was able to think and act positively in the year ahead. The guidance led me to see, as I wrote in my spiritual notebook, June 29, that I "was placing an importance on something really insignificant compared to my central purpose. "Surely," I wrote, "this was needed to deepen my faith, to make me see the mission I am to perform: not to tamper with ecclesiastical machinery in the contest for status—more effectively to preach and teach and heal." And then I wrote this prayer, "O God of hope and love, I praise you who can use this to point my ministry in the right direction. If preferment and honor come, let it be borne with a humility and a love that you can use for your glory and not mine. O Lord, how much it takes of suffering and shock to reveal myself to me. Set me in the right track, O Lord, and keep my spiritual motor running. *Amen.*"

And God did just that! I can truthfully say that I grew more in spiritual maturity in the next twelve months than in any other time of my life. This is guidance by the Spirit, for I certainly could not have done it alone. I did forgive and share that forgiveness with the ones who had wronged me. I began to have a new freedom within that led to freedom in my words and actions. *I can say truly that this hurt and disappointment were one of the best things that ever happened to me! I know that there is always guidance and deliverance when I am open and ready to see and accept it.*

Deliverance from Evil

Christian prayer and worship are indeed the *acceptance of deliverance out of temptation and the victory over the evils of our tests. We find guidance and help in the lost and confused, self-directed, frail, and finite way we must go.* As the petition may be freely translated, "Deliver us from the evil—keep us from having to stand the test we are not able to meet."

Of course we are confused. Life is a bewildering chain of events and circumstances that seem to have no rational or meaningful connection. Certainly the events just described seemed totally unrelated to my conception of life as it ought to be. Nevertheless, the choice is yours, as it was mine, to accept the gift of deliverance out of the evil—the ability to stand whatever tests may come—so that we are not utterly overwhelmed. The gift of deliverance is ours even though we cannot see it at the moment and even though the things we do see declare in human feelings that evil, selfishness, hate, pain, and death are really the rulers. But in spite of all I see, visibly, from the human point of view, I affirm and accept the deliverance that is mine.

This acceptance of deliverance from the oppression of fear, hatred, and despair comes in remarkable ways, primarily and gloriously as by faithful trust we accept the act of God, not only in the risen Christ two thousand years ago, but in God's presence in the Holy Spirit now! "Allowing the resurrected One to be constantly present, I can deal with all the evil suffered by Jesus, by my friends, and by me," witnesses Morton Kelsey, part of whose story was told earlier. "I can face all the rape, pillage, war and hatred that I hear about daily, and still have hope. *The resurrection reveals the ultimate nature of the universe, and the risen Christ continues to give victory over the power of evil.*"[15]

In the chapter in *Resurrection* entitled "A Way of Hope," Kelsey shares more of his own spiritual journey as through vital prayer he was delivered from the darkness of depression.

Sometimes it is as if the darkness seizes me and I have no power of my own to tear myself away from it. . . . Many of us seem to live on the edge of the abyss and the cliffs are constantly crumbling away even when our outer life tells us that we should feel fine. I have discovered that those souls which, like mine, have been worn thin by misery and lack of love as children are open to the direct intrusion of that destructive, down-pulling, befouling spirit which has caused so much misery in our broken and suffering world.

He continues by giving the priceless secret of prayer that accepts the "resurrected One as constantly present":

When I engage my depression rather than trying to run away from it, allow it to be expressed in imaginative pictures or images, and then ask the risen Christ to enter and free me from my inner tormentors, usually I am soon free of the depression. The gruesome darkness retreats and I am accepted and loved by the Christ. Many friends who are attacked in the same way have been lifted out of the pit by this method and enabled to go about the business of life again.[16]

"Preserved from a Thousand Poisons"

Truly this is the experience of countless persons who have learned that by accepting the presence of God they have been delivered from the horrendous evils that threaten them, whether it is depression, discouragement, resentment, hatred for those who have treated them wrongly, or the pains and frailty of the hurts and sorrows of human life. Let me give several more examples of this undeniable fact of human experience which could be summed up in the words of the apostle Paul: "In all these things we are more than conquerors through him who loved us! For I am sure that neither death, nor life, nor angels, nor principalities, nor things present, nor things to come . . . nor anything else in all creation, will be able to separate us from the love of God in Christ Jesus our Lord" (Rom. 8:37–38, RSV).

Let me here point also to the undeniable fact that such deliverance is held in common only by those who live by their disciplined faith. This experience represents something of what the apostle Paul would describe as "Christ in you, the hope of glory" (Col. 1:27, RSV). Disciplined Christians who accept their situations, difficult and costly as they often are, and affirm themselves and their relationship with God find victory. They are "delivered" from the fear and hate and destruction that follows because they know that they are in touch with the reality of eternal love that they have seen in Christ and that is present now in the Holy Spirit. They understand the insistence of Buddha that it is not enough "to know about the ultimate Reality" for to do so is to be compared "to a herdsman of other men's cows." The Christians who know deliverance in the middle of the evil would appreciate the homelier barnyard metaphor of Muhammad, who said that a philosopher who had not experienced his theorizing about the metaphysical (the nature of reality) "is just an ass bearing a load of books." I believe the quality of self-sacrificing love is most fully represented in Jesus Christ. Without this experience of Christlike love known most effectively to those disciplined in the Christian faith, there is little or no hope that people will find life in this age of materialism and high technology. Certainly the devotees of all the great religions, instead of fighting each other, should learn from each other and know that the disciplined way of devotion, which they share in common, must be communicated much more adequately than in the past. For this disciplined way to God is the only hope for the spiritual and moral meanings and unity upon which any true peace and well-being for our human family can depend. Each of us must take the interpretation of that reality that is highest for that individual and seek to interpret it to others. As Christians we must be tolerant of those who cannot yet see all things summed up in Christ!

One good illustration of this kind of deliverance from evil, even while it threatens our most vulnerable point, is found in the story of Ignatius of Loyola, founder of the

Society of Jesus and author of *The Spiritual Exercises*. One day he was asked what he would do if the pope were to decree intolerable restrictions or even an end to his Society of Jesus. He answered immediately, "I would pray about it for fifteen minutes, forget it, and go on." His was a detachment—a "holy indifference"—that did not mean a lack of concern but the fullness of a trusting faith and confidence that he was fulfilling a greater purpose than his own and whatever helped this purpose would not fail!

In the same manner, every victorious spirit has found deliverance out of the most difficult of experiences that had produced new insights, new hope, new strength. In this sense, prayer and the other spiritual disciplines are therefore not an escape or "an opium for the people," as secularists from Karl Marx to the present have called them.

Rufus Jones, the famous Quaker, was for years chairman of the American Friends Service Committee that did so much for the innocent sufferers of World War II, as it has in Vietnam and Korea. Yet his whole life was rooted in the discipline of the Spirit, which brought him through some terrifically difficult times such as the death of his only son, Lowell, and a "nervous breakdown" suffered at the age of fifty. As a result of long periods of overwork, exhaustion, frustration, and no doubt some unresolved emotional problems, this man, who "had been to whole generations the embodiment of optimism, radiant serenity and unbounded energy," found himself at the bottom in "low gear."

"It began to look," his daughter wrote, "as if the cloud would never lift." It took a whole year to regain his strength and his old vim. While lying on the beach in Florida, he remembered the figure of speech used by his friend Violet Hodgkin:

> Isn't it strange how one has to learn to die like a starfish on the beach high and dry and cut off from all renewing while the tide rises and falls *just out of reach*. . . . Then at last, at long last . . . the real spring tide comes and floats

even one's tired out starfish of a body out into the full flood of life again. Only those who know the deadly weariness of the beach can quite understand the living joy of the ocean when we get back to it once more.[17]

How did he come through to such a deliverance from the depression and low tide that may arrive sooner or later to all? His answer no doubt would be similar to his words at the age of eighty-three as his biographer, Elizabeth Gray Vining, visited with him. He sat in a rocking chair on the porch of his home.

Yesterday, I was watching little Willie White playing. He had a wooden duck on wheels which quacked as he pulled it along the driveway. Suddenly something went wrong with the duck, the wheels stopped turning and it stopped quacking. Willie found a soft place on the grass and he lay down on his back and howled. I thought how like the world it was. Something has gone wrong with our duck; it doesn't work anymore; and we lie down on the grass and howl.[18]

Rufus Jones had never done that, even at his worst points in life. Instead, he had experienced the truth of an editorial he had written after his breakdown:

Unusual outside weather is only one of our many means of discipline. . . . Much harder is the fight with inside weather and more dreary and pitiless are the fogs and east winds of our human spirits. . . . The fight with stubborn inward weather, the battle with the devil in us, if you will, is the best kind of fighting there is to be done, and he who has conquered conditions of inner climate has now the best victories which crown men. Not least . . . [is] . . . the further discovery—joyous like that of Columbus sighting a new world—that there are inexhaustible resources of divine grace for those who are resolved to rise above the fog and mist, the sleet and snow of dreary inward weather.[19]

This is surely the wisdom described by Jacques Ellul in the last chapter of his realistic book, *Prayer and Modern*

Man, which he entitles "Prayer as Combat."[20] Prayer is combat with self. It is combat with the symptoms of our sins, such as depression, dejection, and anxiety. It is combat with the false demands of our culture and those around us. It is also combat with God, as we rebel at our circumstances and wrestle as did Jacob at our own river Jabbok until our names are changed and we become "new creations in Christ." This kind of prayer always brings deliverance. It is a million miles from lying in the grass and howling when something is wrong.

Abandonment to Good in the Present Moment

Any person who has such a mature faith, ruling not only the conscious mind but increasingly the depths of the unconscious, accepts deliverance even as one accepts food, health, bread. This person has a trusting faith. J. P. de Caussade, the great French teacher of Christian disciplines, called it *Abandonment or Absolute Surrender to Divine Providence.*[21] This abandonment is the acceptance of myself in the living presence of Christ in every event: in history, in my own life, in every moment, even in the darkest hours, believing that my perspective at this time is inadequate to see it all. Indeed, I can never see more than a very small part of what is. Mine is a knothole view of life as though I were seeing a baseball game through a knothole in the fence. I may see the batter, but I can't see the pitcher; and when a hit is made, I cannot see for the moment whether it is a fly caught in the outfield or a home run.

I can see only a small part of reality, but God sees it all. "Those who are faithful . . . will keep all that I have committed to them against that day" (2 Tim. 1:12, AUTHOR PARAPHRASE). The alternative is a faith that leads to despair in the end. All the great religions of the world deny this except for the secular religions of humanism, communism, materialism, and scientism! Theirs is a faith in the self-sufficiency of humanity, somehow believing the modern fairy tale that, because people can do everything in the physical world of science, they can also conquer their selfishness and greed, their fears and hostility by their own little will. People forget that they may and generally do *will their own* way, which so conflicts with the way of others that the battle is on. Humanity has indeed come to a sad end if, knowing that it is finite, held by a thin rope over the abyss of suffering, pain, evil, death, and nothingness, it feels that *no one* has hold of the other end of the rope!

Alice in Wonderland is a child's story, but a remarkably realistic parable of the progress of human life in our earthly wonderland. It also makes clear the need for a guide to help us through the maze of meaninglessness, hatred, and evil, mixed with such beautiful and treasured goods.[22]

When Alice walks through the looking-glass and finds herself in this bewildering land, everything seems all mixed up. She is utterly confused as she travels through a strange country divided into light and dark patches like a chessboard. There are all kinds of odd people—the mad hatter, a friendly rabbit, a mad queen, and a white knight. She can never see how anything makes sense. But as the story progresses, we see that each of the events that happen to her are "real moves in a real game." They are ways of taking her from her first experience as a pawn to the eighth square, where she would be a queen.

Sometimes the best counsel given seems most foolish, as when the Rose told her to walk away from the Red Queen if she wanted to meet her! (Compare Jesus' paradox of "losing to find.") It is only when she stops out of friendliness to help the silly old White Queen by running after her lost shawl that she jumps over the brook and finds herself on the fifth square. And when she thinks she is hopelessly lost in the dark forest, with only the crazy advice of the White Knight, she is just emerging to her queenship on the eighth square! But through it all the Hand of the Unseen Player is working to help Alice go from being a pawn to a queen!

Life is certainly not a chess game with God as the player and all of us as pawns. That idea is one of the weaknesses of the Muslim approach to the will of God,

as it has been for too many Christians. But our acceptance of the One, who if we let him, "from seeming evil
works good for us," will mean that we grow to be kings
and queens through all the chances and changes of life.
This is the one thing that biographies of the most creative and effective men and women in every age tell us.
Some of these are the anonymous men and women
who, in ordinary ways, are accepting the guidance and
deliverance that keeps them strong and loving, the salt
of the earth and the light of the world!

So when we pray "Deliver us from evil," we are not
asking that trials and tests which are part of our human
lot be reversed. We are asking for deliverance from the
evil tendencies of our self-centered egotism. And
whether we are young or old in years, we need to be
saved from the "old nature," with its cunning disguises
and temptations that cause us to fail in the tests. With
such continued discipline of trust, we accept the step-
by-step guidance and the courage not to be swamped by
the hurly-burly clash of human wills unsurrendered to
anything higher than their own, or by the sudden up-
rush of our own mad-hatter fears and mad-queen likes
and dislikes. We too must walk through the looking-
glass of our own egoistic natural consciousness (the
false shell) into the blazing day of reality. We must get
more and more of our "Me Lens" in focus with the
"Christ Lens," for the more completely we look thus at
ourselves and at others and at the tragedies of evil as
well as the remarkable victories of the good in our
world, the more wonderful is our deliverance from the
evil! For Christlike maturity means that an increasingly
large part of our lives is truly "lived in the Kingdom of
Heaven"—with its blessed heavenly reality!

This may not come to fruition at once. We may not arrive suddenly at the eighth square where we find ourselves king or queen of our own lives. It may not come in
a blaze of sudden light, or even in this earthly life with
all the completeness in store for us. But the symbolic
words of the First Epistle of John declare our unwaver-
ing faith. "How great is the love that the Father has
shown to us! We were called God's children, and such

we are. . . . Here and now, dear friends, we [really] are
God's children; what we shall be has not yet been disclosed, but we know that when it is disclosed we shall be
like him, because we shall see him as he is. Everyone
who has this hope before him purifies himself, as Christ
is pure" (1 John 3:1–3, NEB).

Yes, there are countless temptations and tests that
threaten to pull us aside into the valley of despair and
cynical dejection—the "slough of despond," as Christian called his trials in Bunyan's *Pilgrim's Progress*. There
are tempting times of hedonistic pleasure that offer illusory promises when we seek to make them central. The
pitfalls of such "highs," however arrived at, are the
"morning afters," "the withdrawal symptoms," and the
hours of depression and self-disgust. But we *can* be delivered from these devils in our unconscious minds as
well as from our share of the demons of hate and greed
and selfishness that threaten our homes, our cities, our
world.

The costly freedom to accept or deny is always ours.

> The choice is always ours. Then, let me choose
> The longest art, the hard Promethean way
> Cherishingly to tend and feed and fan
> That inward fire, whose small precarious flame,
> Kindled or quenched, creates
> The noble or the ignoble men we are,
> The worlds we live in and the very fates,
> Our bright or muddy star.[23]

The best and most productive way to make that choice
is in the light of the perspectives and illuminations
when, through prayer, meditation, worship, and other
spiritual disciplines given to us, we center our attention
on Christ. For he is the highest signal we can see of the
exalted yet near reality. The result is the humble, childlike acceptance of the gifts of his bread, forgiveness,
guidance, and deliverance as we give ourselves in loving involvement with the lives of our fellow travelers.

> Oh, at the point where God and man are one,
> Meet me, Thou God; flame on me like the sun;

> I would be part
> Of Thine own heart,
> That by my hands Thy love-deeds may be done:
>
> That by my hands Thy love-truths may be shown
> . . . .
>
> That I may bring
> The dead world spring:—
> The flowers awake, Lord, at Thy word alone.[24]

6

The Disciplines of Caring Love

There is one supreme fact of life that has often been over-looked or forgotten by self-centered, self-sufficient man and woman involved so deeply in self-fulfillment. Whether this quest is through the attainment of our ide-alized self or the satisfaction of our desires and passions in the enjoyment of pleasure, power, possessions, and applause, only at the point where God meets human sons and daughters and unites with us in heart and mind may our hands do the "love-deeds" required for a home, a community, and a world of peace and har-mony. Only where we will the highest will of the God of reality may our minds know the "love-truths" upon which life worth living, indeed, upon which all true self-fulfillment with creative peace and well-being depends.

Prayer and worship and the other spiritual disciplines are the varied means by which we consciously center our attention and train our wills to unite our little lives with the great life of the Mother-Father-God. These dis-ciplines are at their highest and best in the joyous cele-bration of the victory won by the Christ of caring-love on the cross. The victory, however, did not end with Jesus' cross and resurrection. It has been and is now present in the lives of thousands who have caught the spirit of the Son of man and Son of God bearing the cross for others. But it is a celebration that includes more than the emo-tions stirred or the mind enlarged. It is a celebration that leads to the life involved in sacrificial self-giving love with our sisters and brothers in the family of God.

No Separation of the Agony from the Ecstacy

The truth is simple: we all want the ecstasy of being loved and of loving, but we cannot separate the agony of the costs of such love from the ecstasy! That too often Christians and other religious persons have tried to do so and failed is the best commentary on the emptiness and failure of much we call prayer and worship and is the reason for the failure of so many Christians to be Christian enough!

In the preceding three chapters I have sought to interpret and understand how, through the disciplines of the spirit, we may begin to see, to accept, and to become our true selves in the presence of the risen Christ. In the realization of his presence through the Holy Spirit, we lose ourselves in wonder, love, and praise. The wonder and awe we feel as we come to love and trust him is the beginning. The power to love others in joyous self abandonment as God loves us is the continuation and the end of all our longings for a life that is eternal in quality and that never ends. As Bliss Carman declares in the beautiful poem "On Love":

> To love so much, so well,
> The spirit cannot tell
> The range and sweep of her own boundary!
> There is no period
> Between the soul and God;
> Love is the tide, God the eternal sea. . . .
>
> To-day we walk by love;
> To strive is not enough,
> Save against greed and ignorance and might.
> We apprehend peace comes
> Not with the roll of drums,
> But in the still processions of the night.
>
> *And we perceive, not awe*
> *But love is the great law*
> *That binds the world together safe and whole.*
> The splendid planets run
> Their courses in the sun;
> *Love is the gravitation of the soul.*[1]

Jesus' words to his disciples in their last hour together before his agony on the cross declare this awesome truth that love is indeed the first and last requirement for life:

"As the Father has loved me, so I have loved you. Dwell in my love. . . . I have spoken thus to you, so that my joy may be in you, and your joy complete. This is my commandment that you love one another as I have loved you. There is no greater love than this, that a man should lay down his life for his friends. You are my friends, if you do what I command you" (John 15:9–14, NEB).

What Jesus was saying is crucial to our understanding of our new relations with him and with God as "friends." That which is his is ours and our joy is complete! Not that we *must* love him (though that also is true—if we don't learn how to cooperate in love, our civilization and human life itself cannot exist), but we *can love, because we are loved!*

The greatest power in the universe is the joy of Christlike love! As the writer of the First Epistle of John puts it, "God is love, and whoever lives in love lives in union with God and God lives in union with him" (4:16, TEV). "This is what love is: it is not that we have loved God, but that he loved us and sent his Son to be the means by which our sins are forgiven. . . . There is no fear in love; perfect love drives out all fear" (vv. 10, 18, TEV).

This love as God loves is not the possessive 'eros' love that sooner or later always fails, but the Christlike 'agape' giving-love that never fails, as the apostle Paul describes it in First Corinthians 13. A joyful love by which our Father-Mother-Creator gave us life and sent the Son to save us from the destruction of our foolish attempts to make life go according to our own little plans—for that is the essence of our one primary sin.

The Power of Loving Joy

This loving joy in Jesus and in his disciples did indeed turn out to be the most powerful force on earth. It was more powerful than all the bacchanalian orgies of the Caesars, or the orgiastic rites of the Temple of Diana, or

King Louis XIV's or Ludwig II's court, or any pumped up artificial joy in any time or place, including our own hedonistic search for "My pleasure," "My comfort," "My fun," "My fulfillment *first!*"

In my research for the writing of two historical novels relating the story of Onesimus and the early Christians, I have found one certain fact: Christianity conquered the pagan religions of the first and second centuries because the Christian's loving joy, even facing a horrible death, was exhilarating, unmatched by any pagan joy known! Several historians of this period with whom I have consulted agree with T. R. Glover, who summed it up in essence: "They outsang, outlived, outloved and outdied that pagan world!"

It was the power of Christlike love that brought this new joy. We cannot understand the joy of Jesus without the gift of this new power to love! And such love is costly indeed. When we love others as Christ loves us, there is always some agony in the ecstasy. We cannot have the joy without the love, or the ecstasy without the agony!

In 117 A.D. Pliny, governor of one of the Roman provinces, was asked by the Emperor Trajan to investigate the reasons the sect called Christians was spreading so rapidly. In his report he wrote in essence, "One thing above all else characterizes these Christians: the way they love one another!" He could also have said, not only the way they love each other, but the way they love even those who are persecuting them! As Stephen was stoned, he prayed a similar prayer to Jesus' on the cross: "Lord lay not this sin to their charge" (Acts 7:60, KJV). So with thousands who were burned to death or thrown to the lions in the arena. Like Jesus, they prayed for their persecutors.

Is the power of this loving joy possible today? Can we love the terrorists of the Middle East, of Central and South America, of Ireland, or of our own lands? Our own personal enemies who threaten and hurt us? And can we love enough to do the right and best thing required in our situation? The answer of tens of thousands in every age is: *Yes!* We cannot love the evil they do, but we can love them as persons loved by God. Here is the one se-

cret power, unknown to most people, that can overcome
evil when military and economic power are helpless.
*Caring, costly, Christlike love is the only power that can con-
quer the disease of not-caring and remove the unloving joyless-
ness and destruction of selfishness and sin!* This is our good
news! Our giant hope and the hope of all mankind!

*There are countless illustrations of this power of loving joy
"in Christ" over the centuries and today.* As the once unloving and destructive Saul who became Paul the apostle of
love witnessed to the Corinthian Christians, "The love
of Christ leaves us no choice" (2 Cor. 5:14, NEB; "con-
trols us" RSV). And writing to the Colossians, he combined love with joy as no other writer had ever done:
"Now I am happy about my sufferings for you, for by
means of my physical sufferings I am helping to complete what still remains of Christ's sufferings" (1:24,
TEV). What is lacking today? I am sure he would say the
same loving joy!

Perhaps the most dramatic illustration of this ecstasy
in the agony of Christlike love is found in St. Francis
of Assisi. He was a wealthy young playboy in the
eleventh century—another day of materialism and
hedonism. Francis Bernadone, as the son of a wealthy
merchant, leader of young revelers carousing in the
streets, became sick of his empty way of life. To the
amazement of his companions and the disgust of his
father, who disinherited him, he threw off his rich garments and took the rough garments of a peasant. Francis became the troubadour of the loving joy of Christ,
singing and dancing through the streets with his "Little
Brothers," who joined him in pouring out their love on
the poor and needy.

The story of his meeting a leper in the path at the beginning of his new life is representative of the costly joy
of identifying himself with the love of Christ. There was
nothing he loathed more than a leper. He had turned his
horse and started to flee when he remembered how
Jesus in compassion had reached out and touched a
leper. He turned back, took the leper in his arms,
wrapped him in his cloak, and took him to his hut. He
found, to his utter amazement, that "to kiss a leper is to

kiss Christ." Thus, one of the first ministries to lepers was begun.

The best description I know of the combination of love and joy with all the cost involved is found in the great poem by Arthur Shearly Cripps, from "The Death of St. Francis." The poem describes Francis as he identified himself with Christ while praying in a time of solitude on Mount Alvernia. As he prayed he saw a vision of Christ on a huge cross extending over the sky and in his hands and feet he saw the wounds of Jesus. He describes what happened to him:

> How can I tell it? The thing is sacred dear,
> O brothers mine,
> . . . .
> How can I tell?
> . . . .
> His Hands to my hands, Feet of His to mine;
> Exalted and extended on His cross,
> . . . .
> I felt His Heart to beat within my heart.
> It seemed He lent His Sacred Heart to me:
> . . . .
> I knew in blissful anguish what it means
> To be a part of Christ, and feel as mine
> The dark distresses of my brother limbs,
> To feel it bodily and simply true,
> To feel as mine the starving of His poor,
> To feel as mine the shadow of curse on all,
> Hard words, hard looks, and savage misery
> . . . .
> To feel rich brother's sad satieties,
> The weary manner of their lives and deaths,
> That want in love, and lacking love lack all.
> . . . .
> O Heart of Jesus, Sacred, Passionate,
> Anguish it was, yet anguish that was bliss,
> To love them heart to heart, each selfish heart,
> To clasp them close, and pray in utter truth—
> 'Father, forgive, they know not what they do.'
> . . . .
> Was it I that did it? Nay, the Christ in me,
> But when I woke His Prints were in my hands,

> And in my feet, while in my side there showed
> As it were the Heart-Wound from the soldier's
>   lance.[2]

And so with each of us, the way to a life of joy is the way of love that identifies with the love of Christ. Not with the actual marks of the nails in our hands and feet—the stigmata of Jesus—but the bliss that is anguish as "we love them heart to heart" and feel, as our very own, their hurts and sorrows. We join with Christ in bringing healing and wholeness where there has been only sickness and death!

This kind of loving joy embracing the pains and suffering of others has characterized every time of renewal in the church and in human life. In the preceding chapters of this book, we have been seeking to understand the disciplines of the spirit that provide the means by which this identification of the agony with the ecstasy of joyful self-giving love is possible. In this concluding chapter, the description of authentic prayer and worship and fellowship will be further amplified and, I hope, made unmistakably clear.

When Prayer and Worship Are Authentic Celebrations

Today, as in every century, in the words of the Thirtieth Psalm (RSV), God's coming to us by faith "turns our mourning into dancing" and we are filled with the loving joy of our Lord!

One illustration out of many that could be given describing the difference in authentic Christian prayer and worship in our times is the story of Florence Cobb, Christian widow of an Irish policeman. She had a constant fear that her husband would be killed. Though she went with him to worship regularly, her prayers did not remove her fear and hatred for the IRA. One morning an IRA terrorist shot her husband in the back of the head. In her prayers, to her amazement, even in her sorrow and bitterness, she heard the words of her husband and began to say, as he had said to her so many times, "God is stronger than hate! His love is stronger!"

Even in those first awful hours, I did feel an indefinable sense of being cared for. . . .

It was easy, in the days and weeks that followed, to close my ears to these whispers of love. To listen to voices of loneliness, self-pity, depression. And yet in a dozen daily ways, God let me know that He *did* care . . . [through] a friend . . . a letter . . . often from a total stranger.[3]

Then the thought came to her, "Write to Leo"—the man who had shot her husband. She did write to Leo, who now had been imprisoned and was on a hunger strike. The letter wrote itself. "With God's help," she said, "I told him, 'I forgive you.'" She put the letter in the mailbox thinking that was the end of it, but it wasn't. The *Daily Mail* asked for an interview. She told the reporter of her painful three-year adjustment when God became very real to her. Without intending to, she let slip about the letter. "The reporter seemed startled that I had actually written a letter of forgiveness.

"Next morning I was front-page news right across the nation." Television teams came, even from NBC in America.

"It's not *me*," I told them over and over. "It's God's love, seeking a way to Leo."

When the response began to flood in from around the world we marveled again. . . . So many had begun to find healing for their own hurts in the power of "I forgive. . . ."

How can we overcome the hate that threatens to tear us and our world apart? *We* can't. At least, I couldn't. But we can look for signs of God's love at work in this same world—starting as close as our own hearts.[4]

Because her husband knew how to pray the authentic Christian prayer of acceptance and forgiveness in the caring love of God in Christ, she began to pray in the same way. As God became very real to her, she was able to forgive the man who killed her husband and to write the letter that witnessed to the world the power of loving joy! The answer to our deep need for a love that cares and bears and forgives is simple but profound: in the presence of the loving forgiveness of Christ, we too can forgive and we are no longer cursed with "a thousand poisons"!

Indeed, this is our giant hope and the hope of human-kind! This joy, born of love in our living, takes away the fear of dying, removes the cancer of hatred and bitter-ness, and we live no longer on the level of death and de-spair but of life and peace. Then, with Florence Cobb, John Wesley, St. Francis, and all others whose empti-ness has been filled by the love of Christ, we too may become "instruments of his peace."

But let's be realistic: the only way our mourning will be turned to dancing, our hatred into forgiveness, our sorrow into joy is in the presence of the risen Christ, as we discover in our prayerful waiting four glorious facts:

1. We are loved with an everlasting, never-failing love.

2. We can love because we are loved.

3. When by a trusting faith we take the time in per-sonal prayer, reading, study, and meditation and in cor-porate worship and fellowship to accept this love and forgiveness, we too can love and forgive.

4. Then, as we give ourselves caringly and responsi-bly in the use of our time, our money, and energy, we will be able to do the most positive, best thing under the circumstances! Then

> Our mourning is turned into dancing,
> Our despair into hope,
> Our boredom and emptiness into exuberant joy
>   and God's Kingdom comes in us and through us in
>   the world about us!

How Do We Celebrate the Agony with the Ecstasy Through Authentic Prayer and Worship?

Certainly Christian worship must be *enthusiastic* and *joyful*, if it is indeed to be the celebration of the mighty realities of God's caring love in the Christ of yesterday, today, and forever. There are so many good things and pleasures given for us to enjoy that we ought to celebrate them with thankfulness and praise. The lack of this joyous, wholehearted enthusiasm when the good news of life abundant is proclaimed and celebrated in word, act, and song is what makes prayer and worship boring, dull, and dead for so many.

If you find them dull, either as a public or private experience, it is for two simple reasons: there is no sense of the immediacy of the presence of God for you, and, therefore, nothing really happens, even though you are physically present at what is called worship and even though you are pumping up what you hope to be effective prayer.

Christian prayer and worship at their best are keen awareness of and response to the living God who in Christ is present and acting in human life and in all the universe. From the very beginning, Christian worship has been characterized as joyous, meaningful celebration, something to look forward to rather than to avoid. The disciples were taught to worship as Jesus did, by his word and example. They worshiped together not only on the mountain and in homes, but went with him every Sabbath "as was his custom" to the synagogue.

Even on their last night together with its sad and tragic overtones for their finite minds, there was a celebration. "The Lord Jesus on the night when he was betrayed took bread, and when he had given thanks, he broke it, and said, 'This is my body which is for you. Do this in remembrance of me.' In the same way also the cup, after supper, saying, 'This cup is the new covenant in my blood. Do this, as often as you drink it, in remembrance of me'" (1 Cor. 11:23–25, RSV). The disciples did not understand then. Only after the day of Pentecost, when the Holy Spirit came, did they celebrate the Lord's Supper as the Eucharist or thanksgiving for the real presence of their Lord and Master!

This note of ecstasy in the agony—the joy even on the cross—is the most amazing and wonderful fact of our Lord's human experience, as it may be our own. The words of Jesus in the last hour in the upper room are unforgettable. "I have spoken thus to you, so that my joy may be in you, and your joy complete" (John 15:11, NEB). "Peace is my parting gift to you, my own peace, such as the world cannot give. Set your troubled hearts at rest, and banish your fears" (John 14:27, NEB). "But courage! The victory is mine; I have conquered the world" (John 16:33, NEB).

No doubt these words and attitudes of Jesus seemed strangely out of place during the dark hours of the crucifixion and the entombment. They were remembered with fresh meaning as the experiences of his resurrection were known. At Pentecost the disciples at last began to understand, with a tremendous leap of faith, that their friend Jesus was alive in the Holy Spirit—the risen Christ who is the Lord of all creation.

Since Jesus Christ is Lord, there is no agony of human evil and pain too great to be met with the ecstasy of faith and hope. No wonder the note of joy rings throughout the New Testament and in all authentic Christian experience. No wonder that early Christian worship was always a happy occasion. Whether in the "church in their house" or in the catacombs underneath the city of Rome where they met to escape the bloody persecution of a succession of Roman emperors from Nero to Diocletian, their worship was filled with a boundless and overflowing exaltation and delight! Here they celebrated the Eucharist—at daybreak as one of the Roman writers portrayed, "these Christians meet to sing a hymn to Christ as God." This glorious note of celebration is reflected in the book of Revelation. This book contains the only description of worship found in the New Testament. Scholars believe it describes not only the worship in the future at the consummation of God's victory in Christ, but also the way in which the early church celebrated the victory that had already been won in Christ. This celebration was triumphant. Though none could see with physical vision its final consummation, they knew the victory was already there! "But thanks be to God, which giveth us the victory through our Lord Jesus Christ" (1 Cor. 15:57, KJV). "Delight yourselves in God; yes, find your joy in him at all times" (Phil. 4:4, PHILLIPS).

This experience of joyous victory is but a promise of the victory that is to come. "The kingdom of God is near" had been Jesus' recurring theme. The kingdom of heavenly reality is the way things are. The deepest and highest truth of our universe is the rule of Christ at God's right hand—the symbolic way of saying that the Spirit controlling the power behind and through the universe is Christ the Lord! Believing this, Christians have celebrated in words, music, and ritual acts the victory which is now theirs and will be revealed in its fullness in God's good time. For there is "nothing in all creation that can separate us from the love of God in Christ Jesus our Lord" (Rom. 8:39, NEB).

With this in mind, read John's description of the worship of the early church (Rev. 5:11–14, RSV). As you read, seek to translate these ancient symbols into meanings that are as real today as then.

> Then I looked, and I heard around the throne and the living creatures and the elders the voice of many angels, numbering myriads of myriads and thousands of thousands, saying with a loud voice, "Worthy is the Lamb who was slain, to receive power and wealth and wisdom and might and honor and glory and blessing!" And I heard every creature in heaven and on earth and under the earth and in the sea, and all therein, saying, "To him who sits upon the throne and to the Lamb be blessing and honor and glory and might for ever and ever!" And the four living creatures said, "Amen!" and the elders fell down and worshiped.

What does this really mean, beyond the translation of ancient symbols into modern meanings? How do we celebrate the victory—the agony with the ecstasy—in the middle of our confused and chaotic lives? This is the crux of the question of vital prayer and worship.

There is no simple answer, but in this final chapter, I would add as much as I am able from my own experience and my interpretation of the experience of others to an understanding of the disciplines of conscious thought and attention in the use of words, of music, of ritual acts, and of shared silence and study. By these

means our prayer and worship may indeed be true cele-
brations that exalt our vision and bring illumination and
power to our minds and acts. Thus we live in the real
world of technology and of vital personal relationships
with the unseen as well as the seen—but only as our
spiritual disciplines lead us by the love of God to the ecstasy that is never far from the agony of costly, caring
love.

No Joyous Song without Genuine Sacrifice

As a young pastor, I was shocked to hear a great
preacher, Dr. George Arthur Buttrick, say that if we really understood the prayer of our Lord with its demands
for trust and commitment and costly personal involvement with God and God's family in all their evil and sufferings, many, if not most, of us would hesitate or even
refuse to pray it. As it is, too often when we use this
great prayer taught us by our Lord, we rattle it off so fast
that it is without meaning, as are many other of our
"acts of worship." When this happens, our worship is
useless and even harmful.

The last half of this great prayer is as often misunder-
stood as the first half—the obvious reason so many of us
use the words glibly without really praying and acting
on our prayers! For we all want bread, both physical and
spiritual. We all want to be loved, accepted, and forgiven. We want to be led out of temptation that would
really hurt and to be delivered from the evil that could
destroy us. And we want these also for our loved ones
and, in a general sort of way, for others.

*The mighty truth of the rule of God in human life is simple
but immutable: none of these precious gifts are ours unless we
are ready and willing to be involved lovingly and caringly
with others in sharing these gifts.* Surely this is the clear
meaning of Jesus' parable of the final judgment (Matt.
25:31–46). In various other teachings, Jesus made clear
that our receiving forgiveness and mercy are dependent
on our giving forgiveness and mercy.

Unless you care about another's bread you will be
hungry.

The only way you can find forgiveness is to forgive.

The only way to be delivered from evil is as you share with me in delivering others. "For whoever would save his life will lose it; and whoever loses his life for my sake, he will save it" (Luke 9:24, RSV).

That is, if we are to find and share life in the "kingdom of God," we are required by the very nature of our lives in their deepest relationships to recognize and accept the disciplines of Christian prayer and worship. They will become for us a life consciously lived in the perspective of faith in and communion with God, with whom we are involved together in the same loving, redemptive, reconciling task. That is to say, since God the ultimate reality was in Christ reconciling, hugging the world, we cannot be anything less than reconcilers, bridging the gap between ourselves and God as we bridge the gap between ourselves and others. Only then will we pray with our lives, as well as with our words, such a prayer as that of St. Francis, "Lord, make me an instrument of Thy peace."

Dag Hammarskjöld realized this better than most moderns when, in his spiritual diary, *Markings,* he indicated that his own "faith in God demands realization in action: 'In our era the road to holiness (wholeness, maturity) necessarily passes through action.'"[5] But, as Gustaf Aulén, his best interpreter, points out, "this strong accent on action he combines with a similar emphasis on stillness and silence, terms familiar to the mystics. Such quietness does not call only for a pause in a life overspent with work; it calls for constant, restful communion with God in order to find strength."[6] This is not only the *ideal* for humanity, it is the *real*—the only way life will work, either personally, in the family, or in the society of peoples and nations. Whenever we refuse to recognize and pray this prayer and live as we pray, we are going against the grain—we are in hell. As Thomas Merton puts it so vividly:

> Hell is where no one has anything in common with anybody else except the fact that they all hate one another and cannot get away from one another and from themselves.

They are all thrown together in their fire and each one tries to thrust the others away from him with a huge, impotent hatred. And the reason why they want to be free of one another is not so much that they hate what they see in others, as that they know others hate what they see in them: and all recognize in one another what they detest in themselves, selfishness and impotence and agony and terror and despair.

The tree is known by its fruits. If you want to understand the social and political history of modern nations, study hell.[7]

Hence, if one would enter and help his fellows, his home, his country, his world, live in the kingdom of heavenly reality, the first requirement is this commitment in thought and prayer that leads to action by which the caring love of Christ is reproduced in us and through us to our world!

The agony with the ecstasy—but the ecstasy conquers the agony! To be thus involved and equipped for our life and ministry, whether ordained or lay, is indeed the apex and result of Christian prayer at its best. As I have pointed out in several other places, this is not prayer and worship as magical, superstitious hocus-pocus, presumptive attempts to use God for our own exaltation or peace and personal or group security. It is no escape from life—no opiate. Rather it is the opposite: an open-eyed acceptance of life at its best in loving cooperation and fellowship with my brothers and sisters in God's great family. Without this, our prayer and worship are indeed delusions and a curse on us and our fellows.

Caring Involvement: The Summit of Christian Prayer and Worship as Its Conclusion and Result

In this sense, therefore, it is impossible to say where prayer and worship end and work and service begin. Certainly when Jesus put his hands on the eyes of the blind and on the limbs of the lame and leprous, when he held little children in his arms, and when out of love for the loveless and lost of his day and every day he bore his cross to Calvary, he was praying just as when he was alone at the mountaintop.

How strange that we set the one action apart from the other in our lives or in his. Indeed he needed withdrawal to the *solitude* of the desert and mountain without which his return to the valley of *action* and service would have been impossible, or at least ineffective. If the withdrawal was necessary for him, it surely is for us! At the very beginning, he spent forty days and nights, and many other times he withdrew for a whole night in prayer and rest. But remember, his prayer life continued as he came down the mountain and walked out on the common roads of Galilee and, at last, to the cross.

Hence, those who prepare the bulletin for the worship of the gathered congregation must be careful not to put at the bottom of the order of worship, "Worship ends; service begins." For worship is a service to God and man, and service is worship carried to its highest level. Both are required, and he who would do one without the other is running against the cutting edge of the sharp sword or divine-human truth by which life is either enriched and made noble or hurt and destroyed.

Obviously separation of work and worship, prayer and life, is one of the main reasons some people have abandoned prayer and worship as "worn out" and "irrelevant." It is a sad fact that, for many, this kind of prayer and worship has too often been a private piety of escape, a quest for private peace of mind, a culture religion that is a delusion and a curse.

The other side of the story, however, is also true. To be fed, forgiven, led, and delivered from evil by the Lord through the ministry of the gathered community of believers in worship and fellowship and through the personal disciplines of prayer and meditation do give us a priceless peace of mind. Here is the only way to "the peace of God that passes understanding." This is the pathway to courage even in the face of opposition and death. This kind of spiritual discipline does make a nation and a people great and fruitful. But when worship is used primarily for individual or national escape from the demand of caring for others or for false comfort that "is not concerned with the afflictions of Joseph," it is indeed a curse rather than a blessing. That kind of false piety must and will go!

So, if we abandon this false piety, as we must, there is still required a vital piety to take its place—a discipline of prayer, study, worship, and fellowship to supply insight into God's will. Daily strength and courage are required to fulfill it. We must have the discipline to accept the deliverance required from the treacherous enemy of our own self-willed pride with its ugly children of self-pity, envy, prejudice, and hate. We must also accept the victory over those fears and hostilities that result. Such a piety, call it what you will, is the most important of all human disciplines.

One more true story is appropriate here to illustrate the necessity for the kind of spiritual disciplines that seek to let the Spirit of eternal love *use* us rather than the other way round. So often we are like the very self-sufficient, successful sales manager of a large company who had some costly experiences before he learned the difference in the two kinds of piety. He had come to worship occasionally as a member of the church of which I was pastor. When he shook hands with me, it was with the condescending spirit of a wealthy patron who congratulated God and me that he had taken the time from his busy life to attend church. He really did not think he needed worship, much less a discipline of prayer, reading, and meditation. His life had no room for these things that he would leave for weaker men.

At least, so he told me when I first really got to know him. It was on the ninth floor, the psychiatric section, of a large hospital. He had hit the bottom, at last. He had crossed over the line from a compulsive drinker to become an alcoholic. His business relationships were almost ruined. His health was wrecked. His home was on the rocks. His wife and children were through with him. His last shred of self-confidence was gone as he looked up at me with the humble appeal, "Can you help me?"

I answered, as honestly as I knew how, that it all depended on his openness and willingness to learn not just from me but from the Spirit, who was seeking to teach him and lead him through all the suffering he had imposed on himself and others by trying to play God. I explained what this meant, and he responded with great openness to my confession that I had suffered from the same sin he had, only my symptoms were different. I said I had not become an alcoholic—"maybe I would have if I had used alcohol. Perhaps I am a dry alcoholic. But I have other symptoms just as hurtful." I shared with him some of my struggles with envy and jealousy, with hostility toward those who got in my way. Having established a beachhead where both of us were on the same level with much in common, I proceeded to help him draw his own self-picture. We used a chart (see Symbolic Diagram 1) to help make clear that his alcoholism was only a symptom. He had to find the sin. Over a period of weeks, I saw him an hour every two or three days and led him to an understanding of the prayer that brings acceptance, perspective, illumination, and the ability to love. He made the first timid experiment and then wholeheartedly began to pray and to get well. At the same time, I was teaching his wife and two adolescent children something of the same truth and helping them to a reconciliation. It was great indeed to see him and his family reconciled and grow together.

Then he was out of the hospital, taken back to his former job, and, with his family, sitting out in front of me every Sunday. That is, for awhile. Then I missed him. One day I was called back to the hospital and found him flat on his back again.

"What's the matter with me, Lance?" he asked piteously. "I thought I was doing everything you taught me. What went wrong?"

"Well," I asked, "did you continue your prayers? I noticed you have ceased your regular worship."

He apologized for the latter. "I just became too busy, but I didn't stop saying my prayers."

"What were you praying? What did you want in your prayers?"

"I asked God to keep me sober and to help me keep my home and my job," he answered.

"That is, you *used* prayer as a means of *manipulating*

God and God's power to help you keep your old image of yourself and your life and home just as it was. Could that be the reason?"

"I hadn't thought of that. [I realized how little he had understood my previous teaching.] Do you mean that I was trying to *use* God, instead of asking God to use *me?*"

"What do you think?" I countered. "Is this not what Jesus meant when he said, 'Our Father, *your* kingdom come, *your* will be done'?"

He suddenly realized the simple but tragic reason for his failure. In the weeks that followed, he sought to offer up his life where God needed him most. He and his wife became vital, active members of a serving church. He began to find ways to serve those about him. He and his wife are articulate and self-sacrificing followers of the one who came not to be ministered unto but to minister. The difference was a true piety of prayer, worship, and loving action rather than a false use of the forms of devotion as pagan magic, seeking to use God to get and keep a self-exaltation of status and comfort! What a difference!

Who Will Be Willing and Able
to Pay the Cost of Caring?

The answer to this question is the key to the two major problems that confront us as we seek to live an authentic Christian discipleship—a life of ministry, ordained or lay, of caring involvement in the deepest needs and hurts of others. For who really wants to get involved in so costly a way and who really wants to discipline himself?

The answer is, *no one,* unless we have glimpsed at least the beginning of the true perspective of Christian prayer that can enable us to be aware of who we are and what are the promises and resources for us and our fellows in the light of God's loving reality in Christ. Unless we accept the gifts of illumination, courage, and the deep peace of soul that can face the worst having met and conquered our fears, we will avoid getting involved. For "courage is fear that has said its prayers," and certainly we need such courage. Let's face it. None of us wants to get involved in such a costly ministry, and we will not do so unless we have heard God's trumpets of new creation, of judgment and reconciliation every morning!

An old Jewish legend has it that when Satan was asked after falling from heaven what it was he missed most, he answered, "I think what I miss most is the sound of trumpets every morning." God's trumpets every morning are sounding, but only one who is awake to listen and to obey will find the marching orders and the daily rations and the presence of our Captain to lead us on in costly but glorious self-giving! We can take the agony with the joy only in the ecstasy of daily renewed faith! As Evelyn Underhill, the great British teacher of Christian disciplines, declares:

> If the transforming power of religion is to be felt, its discipline must be accepted, its price paid in every department of life; and it is only when the soul is awakened to the reality and call of God, known at every point of its multiple experience, that it is willing to pay the price and accept the discipline. Worship is a primary means of this awakening.
>
> It follows once more that whole-hearted adoration is the only real preparation for right action: action which develops within the Divine atmosphere, and is in harmony with the eternal purposes of God.[8]

So, we might ask, why care for others in their troubles, sufferings, and sins? We might do it in a nice sheltered place in some peaceful valley separated from the roar of human hatred and hell. But this isn't the kind of world we live in. Our world has violence in hearts, homes, and streets and suicidal wars between races and peoples. There is untold suffering in Africa, the Middle East, Latin America, and Asia. Here also is the loneliness of the old woman next door, the cry of hungry children in our ghettos. And don't forget the angry shouts of black and white militants and anarchists and the ma-

jority of middle- and upper-class people anxiously trying to preserve their security with television and money
and not get involved. It seems this is our national goal or
game: how not to get involved. Who really wants to be
God's minister in a world like this if God is not like
Christ? Any natural man or woman in his or her right
mind would not!

No one would want to join in this kind of caring love
unless first of all being hugged by the love of God and
given the assurance of the eternal love ruling all things;
for only such a person can believe in the possibility of
reconciliation and regeneration of human life. Only
such a person will genuinely pray, "Lord, make me an
instrument of Thy peace."

Yes, we must help the hungry to find just plain bread
or help them through their own work; for this is the
bread of God. Unless we are interested in people—their
bodily needs as well as their spiritual—it is unlikely we
will convince them we care for them. Of course the
deepest needs are not physical but spiritual—the hunger for meaning and hope, the thirst for love and courage. So we are involved in sharing these gifts—call it
evangelism or whatever you will. This too is part of
prayer and worship.

This is our highest calling—communicating the intention of our Lord and Savior through our deepest intentions shown in our own acts: "That they might have
life." To pray and worship therefore requires the readiness to be in some humble but real way another incarnation of the love of Christ—to be, as Martin Luther said,
"Little Christs."

"Little Christs!"

One of the mothers in a church in my area told me a
thrilling story that belongs here. She said she noticed
one of the neighbor boys had not been in church school
or worship for two or three Sundays. She asked the
boy's mother why and received this reply: "About two
months ago both of his grandmothers died within a

week. They had taken turns staying with him while I worked. Now he is bereft and refuses to go to church because he says he knows God does not love him or he would not have let his two grandmothers die. I don't know what to tell him." And the young mother herself showed tears in her eyes.

Her neighbor then asked, "Would you tell Mark that I will be glad to be his grandmother if he will let me. This afternoon I will bake some cookies, and you tell him to see me next Sunday."

Next Sunday the little eleven-year-old boy was in his place in church school, and when his neighbor came in, he ran to her and hugged her, and she him. "Oh, will you really be my grandmother? Then God does love me, doesn't he?"

This simple involvement does not seem too costly on the surface, but it will take time and energy, which this dear woman does not really have. Nevertheless, here is the way to pray and to live. Whether it be going as a missionary to Africa, or as a volunteer helper in the ghetto, or as a minister to the poor-rich on mortgage hill, it costs to care. But "Christianity is to Care" as Baron von Hugel put it in his last letter to his niece. "Caring is the greatest thing. . . . Keep your life a life of prayer, dearie. . . . Its [sic] the only thing, and remember, no joy without suffering—no patience without trial—no humility without humiliation—no life without death."[9]

Every one of us has a place and a way to lay our lives on the line, for there are hungry children, youth, seemingly successful adults, and aged in every place, small or large. There are numberless youth crying out for our love and concern. Others are revolting largely because they haven't had anyone to give them love and concern, to listen to them, to care.

How many blind, embittered people are destroying themselves and others! How many youth, as well as those older in years, are still poor in love because no one ever really listened to them? They may not go so far as to run away physically, or to attempt suicide as the affluent young man described in chapter 1. But one point all of them have in common is that no one ever hugged them with accepting love.

Each of us must care deeply about others and their daily bread of both kinds if we would accept our own daily bread of meaning, hope, love, and peace. When you pray, "Give us this day our daily bread," remember that your own children, or your wife, husband, friend, or the lonely man or woman across the street needs this bread of understanding love—someone to listen to, someone to be friendly, someone to care. And what about the children next door and across the tracks and in the inner city, the children in Calcutta and Lima and Kinshasa and Hong Kong?

No, you can't feed them all, nor can I; but we can find a valid ministry wherever we are. *The crucial question is: do you and I encounter the caring love of Christ with such immediacy and adoration that we respond in the joyous prayer of self-giving and the celebration of sacrificial love, so that we may join our caring love with his?* That is the question that will determine the meaning and value of our spiritual disciplines.

We Cannot Do It by Ourselves

One thing is sure: no one is self-sufficient. "No man is an island, entire of itself; every man is a piece of the continent, a part of the main."[10] We are born for community, and belonging is one of our deepest needs. Nowhere is this more true than in the area of spiritual victory over the old self-centered life—the "old man" or "old woman" of self-demands! No one can start *de novo*, isolated from the great stream of human experience in which one may learn from others what a hundred lifetimes on one's own could not teach.

If I am to understand and serve others in caring love, I must understand and know myself. When I pray, "Lead me, but not into temptation," I must have the realism to know what kind of person I am, and not just what I think I am. Without this realistic self-understanding, I may throw myself needlessly into the temptation I cannot or will not resist. Always when an outwardly strong person succumbs to a life-shattering temptation, as happens too often, that person doesn't really know the true self. Nor do companions; that is, there is an aloneness, a separation in "the sounds of silence" of people living together without really communicating.

And so the friends or family say, "What's wrong?" "How could that have happened?" Neither the person nor family and friends understand the factors that affect the person's judgment, the prejudice and group satisfactions to which that person is subject, the longing for status and acceptance which has deep roots, unrecognized but powerful.

There are things about myself I need to know and understand if I am to grow into the maturity of the new person in Christ. This self-knowledge is hard to come by and *never* is it found alone. I may find some help through psychology, group therapy, sessions with a psychiatrist, and it must be said with confidence that the Spirit works through these media as well as through the professedly "religious" counselor, friend, or group. The most powerful help comes from the Christian koinonia or fellowship meeting for prayer, sharing, and study together.

Most maturity comes in open-minded honesty before the God who knows me as I am—an honesty which may be helped by the group in which I share, but in the last resort the light on who I am at best is given me when I open up every corner of my being to his light. It comes when I cease to trust my own competence or strength, but pray "I can do all things through God who gives me power. Without God I can do nothing. Show me my false shell and lead me to the person I am in your sight." There is no substitute for this kind of prayer and the celebration in worship that declares jubilantly, "For yours (not mine) *is* the *Kingdom* and the *power* and the *glory, forever* and *ever,* amen!" Only then will my celebration in solitude and in the gathered community enable me to be free really to care intelligently for my family, my church, and humankind.

Life Together

However, even in the solitude of my personal prayers, as well as in the corporate worship of the church (the koinonia of the early Christians that still exists in powerful reality here and there in the Christian church), *I must have group support and guidance, a group in which I join in the acceptance of Christlike disciplines.* Here in this matter of our "life together," as Dietrich Bonhoeffer calls it, is the final discipline without which the others will be empty and fruitless. Strangely enough, it is the one discipline most neglected today. Bonhoeffer, though in a Nazi prison awaiting execution, continued strong to the end not only because of his personal meditation and prayer, but because he was supported by a group of loving friends in and out of prison. He wrote:

> This is the test of true meditation and true Christian community. Has the fellowship served to make the individual free, strong, and mature, or has it made him weak and dependent? Has it taken him by the hand for a while in order that he may learn again to walk by himself, or has it made him uneasy and unsure? . . . Blessed is he who is alone in the strength of the fellowship and blessed is he who keeps the fellowship in the strength of aloneness.[11]

This Bonhoeffer knew from experience. The disciplines of personal prayer and meditation must be balanced by the discipline of group silence, fellowship in dialogue and study and celebration through corporate worship. Douglas Rhymes has a sentence that needs to be written in large letters over our churches, schools, homes, and places of work and play: "A society without any disciplines is unable to provide the right environment for freedom, for the resultant anarchy will simply produce a jungle in which the more sensitive go to the wall."[12]

This is what has happened to many homes and churches where young, middle-aged, and old are alone, even in what is supposed to be a community. We need the disciplines of a group in which we truly can belong and in which we are able both to listen and to contribute. Without these, we will find, in our society and in our inner lives, an anarchy where the most sensitive go to the wall and the strongest are the most predatory and destructive! How many homes and churches are more likely to resemble a barnyard of squabbling dogs and cats, pigs and chickens than a family where the peace and love of Christ dwells!

We need a *koinonia* as did Jesus and his disciples, whom he chose "that they might be with him." If they needed it we certainly do—this beloved fellowship where we are "speaking the truth in love" (Eph. 4:15, RSV), where when one has slipped, all the others join to "restore him in a spirit of gentleness. Look to yourself, lest you too be tempted. Bear one another's burdens" (Gal. 6:1–2, RSV). And yet "each man will have to bear his own load" (Gal. 6:5, RSV).

How do we get such a fellowship? It doesn't just happen, but it is given to those who seek it through disciplined group worship and study, the practice of silence and sharing together, "each one considering the other as better than himself." This requires a corresponding discipline of our individual lives in our times of solitude, for such community of openness and helpfulness to each other requires a genuine humility in the presence of Christ where "we compare ourselves with ourselves and not with one another" (cf. 2 Cor. 10:12–17). Instead, we compare ourselves with Christ and the self he knows we are and can be; then only will we be strong and wise enough to share the bread of God, the forgiveness, healing guidance, and deliverance God is seeking to bring through us to our brothers.

The warning of Dietrich Bonhoeffer is needed by us all: "Let him who cannot be alone beware of community. . . . Let him who is not in community beware of being alone."[13] For if you attempt to escape from the aloneness in which you see yourself and come to grips with who you are and can be in the presence of God, your presence in the community will only do harm to yourself and the community. On the other hand, unless you are accepted, loved, supported, and guided by the community, your aloneness will bring you to all kinds of illusory leadings and false exaltations or equally false depressions.

The disciplines of solitude and community belong together. Without them and the light and leading they bring, we can never celebrate the agony with the ecstasy and find ourselves able to join in the joy of self-giving love.

> Man . . . will make the choice between arrogant autonomy and loving excentration. This will be the final choice: revolt or adoration of a world.[14]

Colin Morris, former president of the United Church of Zambia, has a little book called *Include Me Out!* that points up the choice each of us must make. He wrote it on the very day he received a copy of the *Methodist Recorder* telling about all the minutiae of working out the proposed union between British Methodists and the Church of England. On the very same day, a poor, starving Zambian died on his doorstep with only a few leaves and a ball of grass in his stomach. As Dr. Morris read and thought about the two events, he wrote, "Include me out!" He does not mean, as he hastens to indicate, "Include me out of union," for he does not believe we should quit working toward a union of our forces as Christians in a pagan world. His theme is rather *include me out of worship or prayer or any other emphasis in the church and in my life that fails to put the deepest needs of people first.* Count me out of worship and prayer that omits the major concerns of compassion, how to share with our neighbors who are starving for want of food and love. Colin Morris's little book contains a classic description of the kind of corporate worship that results when men and women are celebrating the self-giving love of their Lord by joining with God in their own action and love.

> The worship of men and women spending themselves in compassionate action would have an air more of des-

peration than formality. They would stagger into
Church utterly drained of goodness, unable to face another day unless their numbed spirits were resensitized
and their strength renewed. . . . Every false word in the
service would stick out like a sore thumb . . . the most
familiar truth would scorch. They would gulp the bread
of Communion like starving men. . . . And they would
not casually go through the motions of a ritual expecta-
tion of Resurrection on that first day of the week. There
would be a heart-stopping suspense as the service progressed. Would they really find a Risen Lord at work in
the heart of the tragic mess to which they would have to
return?[15]

And they would leave with their spirits renewed and
their hearts overflowing, for they had celebrated with
the faithful of all ages the presence of *Christus Victor*.

Thus it has been in every day and every time, and
thus it will be for those who share in the victory that can
truly make this the kingdom of heaven! "The sover-
eignty of the world has passed to our Lord and
his Christ, and he shall reign for ever and ever" (Rev.
11:15, NEB).

So let us join with Jesus and his disciples in every age
who are caringly involved in self-giving love with the
Lord of History:

Count me in wherever Christ is at work in loving reconciliation.

Count me in wherever my brothers and sisters meet for
worship and study as we seek together to discover the will
of God in these perplexed times.

Count me in when the celebration of the Presence is held,
the bread for which I hunger is offered, the wine of love
and hope for which I thirst is poured out for me and for all.

Count me in on these set-apart days of solitude where I
can get my bearings as I am surrounded by a great cloud of
witnesses.

Count me in as I join with others who cry daily, hourly,
momently, "Your kingdom come, your will be done . . . for
yours is the kingdom, the power and the glory!"

Count me in with the myriad upon myriads who stand
around the throne of highest reality crying, "Alleluia!
Amen—Yes" to the One who reigns in caring love and
shall forever reign, "King of Kings and Lord of Lords forever!"

All of life, then, is a sacrament of the unseen reality of
God's presence, that is, the invisible becomes visible in
the experienced joys and pleasures of the common life,
in heroic sacrifices, and in the patient bearing of our burdens as we share with God the burdens of others.

Yes, "awe alone is sterile. But when it is married to
sacrificial love, the fruits of the Spirit begin to appear."[16]

> The god of galaxies—how shall we praise him?
> For so we must, or wither. Yet what word
> Of words? And where to send it, on which night
> Of winter stars, of summer, or by autumn
> In the first evening of the Pleiades?
> . . . .
>   oh, what word
> Of words? Let us consider it in terror, [and in joy!]
> And say it [with and] without voice. Praise universes
> Numberless. Praise all of them. Praise Him.[17]

The disciplines required for life in our age of dimmed
hope, doubt, and despair are the ones that celebrate the
marriage of awe and love, of worship and work and joyful living, all in the awareness and response to the God
who in Christ "is hugging [us,] the world [and the
whole universe] to himself" and calling us to join in the
glorious celebration.[18]

NOTES

Chapter One: Two Ways to Life

1. Edward Sanford Martin, "My Name Is Legion," in *Masterpieces of Religious Verse,* ed. James Dalton Morrison (New York: Harper & Brothers, 1948), 274.

Chapter Two: Buckets for the Well of Life

1. William Cowper, *The Task,* Book 3, "The Garden," line 188.
2. Albert Outler, *Sermons of John Wesley,* Vol. 1, No. 17 (Nashville, TN: Abingdon), 376.
3. Maxie Dunnam, *Alive in Christ* (Nashville, TN: Abingdon, 1982), 26.
4. Harry Emerson Fosdick, "The Sense of God's Reality," *The Christian Century,* 6 Nov. 1919; reprint, *The Christian Century,* 4–11 July 1984, 677. Italics added.
5. Dag Hammarskjöld, *Markings* (New York: Alfred A. Knopf, 1964), 198.
6. Gustaf Aulén, *Dag Hammarskjöld's White Book* (Philadelphia: Fortress Press, 1969), 84.

Chapter Three: The Basic Disciplines of True Perspectives

1. Maxie Dunnam, *Workbook on Spiritual Disciplines* (Nashville, TN: The Upper Room, 1984), 8.
2. Richard J. Foster, *Celebration of Discipline* (New York: Harper & Row, 1978).
3. Albert Edward Day, *Discipline and Discovery,* rev. ed. (Nashville, TN: The Parthenon Press, 1976), 17.
4. Quoted by Douglas V. Steere in *The Hardest Journey* (Lebanon, PA: Sowers Printing Co., Pendle Hill Pamphlet No. 163, 1969), 9–10.
5. C. G. Jung, *Psychology and Alchemy,* vol. 12 of *The Col-*

lected Works (Princeton, NJ: Princeton University Press, 1953), 11–12. Italics added.

6. Stanley Hauerwas and William H. Willimon, "Embarrassed in God's Presence," *The Christian Century,* 30 Jan. 1985, 98.

7. Lance Webb, *On the Edge of the Absurd* (Nashville, TN: Abingdon, 1965), 74–75.

8. Hammarskjöld, 105.

9. Arthur Koestler, "A Conversation with Arthur Koestler and Elizabeth Hall," *Psychology Today,* June 1970, 63.

10. Edward Schillebeeckx, *Christ the Sacrament of the Encounter With God* (New York: Sheed and Ward, 1963), 14–15.

11. Thomas E. Clarke, S. J., "Can Man Encounter God Today," in *Prayer: The Problem of Dialogue With God,* ed. Christopher F. Mooney, S. J. (Paramus, NJ: Paulist Press, 1969), 13.

12. Ibid.

13. Ibid., 17.

14. Ibid., 13.

15. For the difference in "desiring-love" and "giving-love, see Lance Webb, *How Good Are Your Virtues?* (Nashville, TN: Abingdon, 1983).

16. Alan Paton, *Instrument of Thy Peace* (New York: Seabury Press, 1968), 7.

17. Ibid., 11–12.

Chapter Four: The Costly Disciplines of Illumination

1. Clarke, 14. Italics added.

2. Matthew Fox, *Breakthrough: Meister Eckhart's Creation Spirituality in New Translation,* Introduction and commentary by Matthew Fox (Garden City, NJ: Image Books, 1980), 223.

3. Howard McKinley Corning, "Pruning Vines," in *Modern American Poetry,* 6th rev. edition, ed. Louis Untermeyer (New York: Harcourt, Brace and Company, 1942), 574.

4. David M. Stanley, S. J., "Contemplation of the Gospels," in Mooney, 55.

5. Ibid., 73. Final italics added.

6. Ibid., 56–57.

7. Ibid.

8. Frederick W. Faber, "There's a Wideness in God's Mercy," Hymn.

9. Alfred Lord Tennyson, "The Higher Pantheism," in *The Complete Poetical Works of Tennyson* (Boston: Houghton, Mifflin Company, 1898), 273.

10. Viktor E. Frankl, *Man's Search for Meaning* (Boston: Beacon Press, 1952).

11. D. H. Lawrence, "Thought," in *The Complete Poems of D. H. Lawrence*, vol. 2, ed. Vivian de Sola Pinto and F. Warren Roberts (New York: Viking Press, 1964), 673.

12. Evelyn Underhill, *The Spiritual Life* (New York: Harper & Row, 1936), 67.

13. Douglas Rhymes, *Prayer in the Secular City* (Philadelphia: Westminster Press, 1967), 31–32.

14. Thomas R. Kelley, *A Testament of Devotion* (New York: Harper & Brothers, 1941), 65.

15. Thomas à Kempis, *The Imitation of Christ*.

16. Lance Webb, *How Bad Are Your Sins?* (Nashville, TN: Abingdon, 1962), 25–43.

17. See Lance Webb, *The Art of Personal Prayer* (Nashville, TN: Abingdon, 1962), 25–43.

18. Aulén, 80.

19. Hammarskjöld, 104.

20. Aulén, 80.

21. Walter Rauschenbusch, "The Postern Gate," in *Walter Rauschenbusch* by Dores Robinson Sharpe (New York: Macmillan, 1942), 451.

Chapter Five: The Joyful Disciplines of Acceptance

1. Morton Kelsey, *Resurrection: Release from Oppression* (New York: Paulist Press, 1985) 12–14.

2. Ibid., 15.

3. Ibid., 17.

4. Ibid., 19.

5. John Greenleaf Whittier, "Snow-Bound," in *New Oxford Book of American Verse* (New York: Oxford University Press, 1976), 117.

6. See "Christian Perfection," in *Works of John Wesley*, ed. Albert C. Outler (Nashville, TN: Abingdon, 1980), 2:97-124.

7. Mark Twain, *The Adventures of Huckleberry Finn* (New York: The Heritage Press, 1940), 24.

8. Paul Vitz, *Psychology as Religion: The Cult of Self-Worship* (Grand Rapids, MI: Eerdmans, 1977).

9. Aaron Stern, *ME: The Narcissistic American* (New York: Ballantine Books, 1979).

10. Henri J. M. Nouwen, *The Way of the Heart* (New York: Seabury Press, 1981), 71–75. Italics added.

11. See "Working Out Your Own Salvation," in *The Works of John Wesley,* vol. 7, ed. Thomas Jackson (Erdman's Publishers, 1872).

12. "What Wondrous Love Is This," American Folk Hymn.

13. John Henry Cardinal Newman, "The Pillar of the Cloud," in *19th Century Minor Poets,* ed. W. H. Auden (New York: Delacourte Press, 1966), 125.

14. Francois de Fénelon, *Christian Perfection* (New York: Harper & Brothers, 1947), 41.

15. Kelsey, 19. Italics added.

16. Ibid.

17. Elizabeth Gray Vining, *Friend of Life* (Philadelphia: Lippincott, 1958), 150–51.

18. Ibid., 304–5.

19. Ibid., 153.

20. Jacques Ellul, *Prayer and Modern Man* (New York: Seabury Press, 1970), 139ff.

21. J. P. de Caussade, *Abandonment or Absolute Surrender to Divine Providence* (New York: Benzinger Brothers, 1887, 1945).

22. See Evelyn Underhill, *Abba* (New York: David McKay, 1960). 73–75.

23. Aldous Huxley, "Orion," in *The Cicadas and Other Poems* (London: Chatto & Windus, 1931), 39.

24. George Barlow, "The Immortal and the Mortal," in *The Oxford Book of English Mystical Verse,* ed. D. H. S. Nicholson and A. H. E. Lee (London: Oxford University Press, 1917), 372–73.

Chapter Six: The Disciplines of Caring Love

1. Bliss Carmen, "On Love," in *Oxford,* 457–58. Italics added.

2. Arthur Shearly Cripps, "The Death of St. Francis," in *Oxford*, 513–16.

3. Florence Cobb, "Healing the Hurts," in *Guideposts*, July 1985, 4.

4. Ibid., 6.

5. Hammarskjöld, 122.

6. Aulén, 119.

7. Thomas Merton, *Seeds of Contemplation* (Norfolk, CT: New Directions Books by James Laughlin, 1949), 60.

8. Underhill, "Abba," *Fruits of the Spirit, Light of Christ, and Abba:* Meditations Based on the Lord's Prayer (New York: David Mckay, 1956; *Abba* copyright 1940), 24.

9. Gwendolyn Greene, Introduction to *Letters to a Niece* by Friedrich Von Hugel (London: Dent, 1928), xlii.

10. John Donne, *Devotions*, XVII.

11. Dietrich Bonhoeffer, *Life Together* (New York: Harper & Brothers, 1954), 88–89.

12. Rhymes, 45.

13. Bonhoeffer, 77.

14. Pierre Teilhard de Chardin, *The Future of Man* (New York: Harper & Row, 1964), 19.

15. Colin Morris, *Include Me Out!* (Nashville, TN: Abingdon, 1968), 36–37.

16. Underhill, *Abba*, 25.

17. Mark Van Doren, "The God of Galaxies," in *Collected and New Poems 1924–1963* (New York: Hill and Wang, 1963) 437–38.

Lance Webb, a bishop in the United Methodist church, is retired from administrative responsibilities. Before his election to the office of bishop, he pastored two large university churches in Texas and Ohio for a total of twenty-four years. During his career, Bishop Webb has blessed many through counseling and through teaching about prayer. He is currently a consultant on spiritual formation with The Upper Room. In addition, Bishop Webb is active in leading seminars, workshops, and retreats for both clergy and laity.

Bishop Webb is the author of numerous books, including *The Art of Personal Prayer, God's Surprises, Making Love Grow, On the Edge of the Absurd,* and *Onesimus,* a historical novel of the apostle Paul and the early church. Lance Webb and his wife Elizabeth now reside in Dallas.